WIND ON THE BUFFALO GRASS

Books by the author

The Fall of the Aztecs
American Needlework 1776–1976
Wind on the Buffalo Grass

WIND ON THE BUFFALO GRASS:

The Indians' Own Account of the Battle at the Little Big Horn River, & the Death of their life on the Plains

collected and edited by

LESLIE TILLETT

Thomas Y. Crowell Company
Established 1834   New York

Designed by Margaret Dodd

Manufactured in the United States of America

Library of Congress Cataloging in Publication Data

Tillett, Leslie, 1915-
    Wind on the buffalo grass.

    Includes index.
    1. Little Big Horn, Battle of the, 1876. I. Title.
E83.876.T54   973.8'2   76-6098
ISBN 0-690-01155-5
ISBN 0-690-01188-1 (Limited edition)

10 9 8 7 6 5 4 3 2 1

Kills Two is the artist who did the sketches reproduced
opposite the title page and on the facing page. The latter
depicts the old style of dog travois used by the Indians
before the coming of the pony in the 17th century.

To Doris, Dek, Linnaea, and Seth

ACKNOWLEDGMENTS

So many people have helped so much in the compiling of this book that it is impractical to name them all. However, David Humphreys Miller, The Rio Grande Press, Inc., and The University of Nebraska Press have been particularly helpful.

I want to thank Lloyd Kiva New for his encouragement and fine introduction.

Most important has been the help and dedication of my assistant, Victoria Negrin.

CONTENTS

INTRODUCTION

I am pleased to have this opportunity to express my views about the timeliness of *Wind on the Buffalo Grass.*

Though that battle has been covered, seemingly from all angles, most of the material I have seen does not depart far from the typical interpretation concerning General George Custer's misplaced ego and his underestimation of the enemy, which together resulted in a melee that has gone down in history as the Indian battle with the most surprising of endings. What happened at the Little Big Horn will always titillate those who take satisfaction in seeing the underdog win a few, but the incident has special interest to many others because of their enduring interest in the social issues of contemporary minority groups. To Indians, that battle will serve forever as the classic example of one time, at least, when the Great Spirit came through in proper fashion.

With the neo-Indian wars going on in the Dakota country, Wounded Knee II, the trials of the Indian defendants, and the most recent confrontations between Indians and FBI agents, this is a very good time indeed to rethink the entire matter of Indians in America—on this coming hundredth anniversary of the Battle at the Little Big Horn River and, ironically, on the Bicentennial of the beginning of the process that eventually dispossessed Indians of many of their freedoms and possessions.

Wounded Knee II and other recent events are precursors of similar sporadic uprisings that will occur as Indians and other minority culture groups continue to grope for effective ways to express new nationalistic postures now being supported by changing worldwide attitudes in favor of racial and cultural pluralism. Embers of the fires of conflict presumed to be dead since the cessation of the open wars of the 19th century still smolder in the minds of many Indian people. These embers will be fanned into life at intervals so long as that people's need for cultural and political recognition is not satisfied.

Fortunately for all concerned, a subtle shift seems to be underway in which so-called "primitive culture" groups are gaining new levels of recognition over those afforded during the darker periods when cultural colonialism was practiced so relentlessly. Indeed, there appears to be a growing interest on the part of "progressive" groups in reinterpreting some of the values held by other cultures to determine whether they hold new or forgotten clues about man's basic relationship to nature—clues of a kind that could be used to assist them in their efforts toward extended survival. It is already known that the arts of "primitive" groups serve as a continuing wellspring and inspiration to all of contemporary mankind—there are other messages as well.

Although this magnificent volume presents an extensive collection of drawings and paintings done by Indians of scenes from the battle, as well as little-known quotes from some of the Indian participants, it will not be the definitive antidote to all the superficial Wild West versions of that famous event. It will however give a preprogrammed 20th-century audience the opportunity to see some fascinating and exquisitely executed Indian art in connection with one of the classic turnabout events in the history of Indian/white relations.

For many years I have lamented the loss accruing to both sides from the fact that only a very few people know about the existence of Indian paintings and drawings of the Battle at the Little Big Horn River—paintings that comprise some of the most effective artistic statements in the history of Indian art. It is high time that the general public had an opportunity to see a famous (or infamous) event in history portrayed in the manner that will overcome the generally vacuous coverage given to the Native American side of stories coming out of that period of American history.

But most important, the book shows the Indians as a reverent, sensitive people whose fine artists drew on their ancient and rich culture. Their splendid pictures reveal the injustice of the unprovoked attacks of the whites, and, when underlined by the actual accounts of the various participants, they make *Wind on the Buffalo Grass* a vital force for changing commonly held historical views and the greater weight of public opinion.

Lloyd Kiva New
Director, American Indian Art Institute

PREFACE

Between the last European war and the horrors of the war in Indochina, the level of general awareness about racial oppression has dramatically changed. We understand genocide now. We have seen its results. We know what the destruction of a people and their culture can be, and we have all "communicated" with the racial sufferings of the Third World. Our new awareness makes us finally see what we have done, and are still doing, to the First Americans.

I am trying here to show the Plains Indians as artists, but must show them as artists working in a world of continuing injustice.

The idea of building a book around the Battle at the Little Big Horn River came to me last year, during a visit to the Sioux headquarters in Bismarck, North Dakota. I was talking about the U.S. Bicentennial when one of the Sioux leaders asked, "What about our centennial the same year?" It took a moment for me to realize they were talking about the Battle, which is to them the most important single event in their history, and a date by which they measure other events. Having discovered and bought two portfolios entitled *Sioux Indian Painting* twenty years ago, I have wanted for some time to do a book on the art of the Plains Indians. During that time I have worked closely with Indians and lectured at the American Indian Art Institute in Santa Fe. Through contact with the students, my awareness of the Indians' anger and resentment grew, and once joined with my respect for their fine art abilities, inspired me finally to undertake the project which produced *Wind on the Buffalo Grass.*

Taking the Battle as the pivotal point, I saw that I could present it only in the context of what the Indians of the Plains were fighting for. To do this involved first exploring the main aspects of the Indians' way of life, best described through their own art. This would have been difficult without the help of Eagle Lance, or, as white men called him, Amos Bad Heart Buffalo.

The almost accidental finding of his ledger sketchbook in 1927 by Helen Blish must rank as a most important discovery in American Indian research. It was in the possession of his sister Dolly Pretty Cloud, who had had it since Amos's death in 1913. With great foresight, Helen Blish had it photographed while she was studying it—when Dolly died in 1947, the sketchbook was buried with her forever, as disinterment is prohibited by the Indians. Many of the drawings in this book were done by Amos, although I have used other Indian artists' work as well.

The brief comments attached to most of the pictures of "daily life" say enough about the life style of the Plains Indians for the purpose of this book, which is to let the pictures tell the story. It is well simply to keep in mind that the Indians (particularly the Sioux) were a nomadic people who moved their encampments to follow the buffalo, or to find fresh pasture for their ponies, or, occasionally, to relocate as a result of tribal wars. If the history of man can be simplistically understood as the change from food gathering to hunting, and then to farming and finally industry, we can see the Plains Indians as the last great hunters, living on into the industrial era.

I have divided the pictures of daily life into scenes of migration, hunting, war, love, and ceremony; but, of course, one cannot separate these activities. The ceremonies were concerned with war and hunting, and they went on amidst the necessities of the Indians' migratory life.

It is more important to give some background about Custer's part in the Battle of the Little Big Horn than to describe the movements that took place on the battlefield. Custer was the most written-about "boy general" of the Civil War, and virtually all the details of his exploits have been published at some time. His wild cavalry charges against all odds had nearly always resulted in victory; so no one ever questioned the constant large losses of the men who rode with him. He was in fact an avid but somewhat lighthearted headline hunter throughout the Civil War. He brought this style to the Indian Wars, but there, the glory he sought became a grim necessity in the face of low pay and political intrigues. It seems beyond doubt that he meant to make the kind of headlines that could put his name high on the list of Democratic contenders for the Presidency. The convention was less than a week away on June 25, and Custer had a reporter from the *Tribune* with him, which was against orders. He had also had significant talks in Washington and New York before arriving for this campaign. He talked to his scouts about what he could do for them if he became the "great white father" in Washington. All this cannot be proven, and is admittedly hearsay, but it amounts to more than circumstantial evidence. Custer has been much criticized for splitting his small regiment into three battalions, and critics see this as one more of his attempts to grab a bit of glory and another headline. It should be remembered, however, that the greatest problem of the general was to get the Indians to hold still while they were being killed. Always outgunned, the Indians knew, as did the North Vietnamese of recent memory, that their hope lay in guerilla tactics. General Terry had been adamant with Custer about "cutting off their escape." Therefore, it is understandable that Custer sent Benteen around the Wolf Mountain hill to block any escape to the Southeast, and sent Reno into one end of the village while he planned to attack from the other. It has also to be remembered that the basic tactic was to attack the village encampment, killing the women and children, so that the warriors would have to fight in the open to defend them. With their repeating rifles against the Indians, most of whom had only bows and arrows, and the rest old single-shot rifles with little ammunition, it seemed that the soldiers needed only to get the enemy into the sights of their rifles. Custer attacked a numerically overwhelming force of Indians with blind courage, but that blindness defeated him. He did not know how many, nor under what chiefs, the Indians were fighting. To charge into some 4,000 warriors under such inspired leaders as Crazy Horse and Sitting Bull, who were suddenly put to the test of defending their women and children, was madness.

The aftermath of the Battle at the Little Big Horn River had to be included in this book because it is in this aftermath that we all live. A nation of 40 million, tempered by the Civil War, and once more united in its westward expansion, was celebrating its centennial when the news of the Custer defeat was received. The idea that these ragamuffin bands could stop the spread of "Civilisation" and "manifest destiny" was impossible to accept; that they could defeat a part of the U.S. Army under the national hero, General George A. Custer, was even more incredible. And finally, the fact that the Indians had stripped and mutilated the bodies, and escaped almost unharmed, gave the "exterminate the Indians" faction all they needed. The small voices of humanity and compassion were hushed by an angry shout for revenge, a shout that echoed back to the Black Hills, where gold could make revenge profitable as well. That great leader Crazy Horse was assassinated in a most brutal and ignominious way in 1877. After that followed twelve years of rapid decline of any hope left the Indians. This emotional people of the Plains succumbed to the wild hopes embodied in the promise of the Ghost Dance.

Wovoka, a Paiute, was given the credit for starting the whole movement of Ghost Dancing. His father had been a sort of messiah medicine man. He had inherited the mantle, and added some ideas of his own. The Indians had always believed wholly in the resurrection of the spirit—the Ghost Dance movement capitalized on this belief. The Ghost Dance was a ritual in which central dancers in touch with the legions of the dead could communicate, and essentially "bring power," to the living. That power from the departed would scatter the white hordes into nothingness. It would bring back the buffalo herds. Ghost Dancing as a means of invoking the spirits to these worthy ends swept through the Plains Indian tribes. Because of their hunger and their misery, a frenzy grew that was feared by the white custodian-jailers. Sitting Bull and his men, as the natural leaders, were assassinated before they could cause trouble. The brutal massacre at Wounded Knee followed, and broke the spirit of the Plains Indians. But it was not broken forever. The new militant Indian groups are working hard and boldly to bring the whole Indian question to the consciousness of us all. The descendants of those killed at Wounded Knee are now suing the United States government.

Our literature is just beginning to hint at the reality of the Indian position, but it will take a great rain of truth to wash away the layers of ignorance and hostility that have accumulated in the white American mind. The truth of the Indian situation is buried under strata laid down by Hollywood films and bad books, and these strata will not dissolve overnight. But a more honest attitude does seem to be spreading, and it is my modest hope that in the reassessment, my book will be of some help. Seeing the Indians as artists who depict their own life style and battles will help, we hope, to put majority opinion on their side in this struggle for respect and fair treatment. In a book that attempts to give the Indians' side of history by presenting their art and quoting their words, I have not wanted to include any white man's words but these by President John F. Kennedy:

> It seems a basic requirement to study the history of our Indian people. America has much to learn about the heritage of our American Indians. Only through this study can we as a nation do what must be done if our treatment of the American Indian is not to be marked down for all time as a national disgrace.

The Sioux had a saying: "A people without history is like wind on the buffalo grass." History was important to the Indian tribes, and in each community a recorder, or band historian, was appointed who could draw the necessary pictographs with complete objectivity. In the time of dissolution, when all their traditional ways were crumbling before the white man, Amos Bad Heart Buffalo (born 1869, died 1913) became the band historian of his tribe, the Oglala Sioux. He inherited this position from his father, but his main informants were his two uncles, He Dog, a great warrior and leader ("shirtwearer"), and Short Bull (Tatanka Pacela). Amos's father, known as Bad Heart Bull the Elder, and He Dog were the chief informants of Helen Blish, who compiled the fine manuscript "A Pictographic History of the Oglala Sioux—illustrated by the work of Amos Bad Heart Buffalo."

Art was not the province of the band historian alone; everyone in the Sioux communities was an artist of some sort, and had to learn to draw as well as read the picture messages, or inscriptions, left on buffalo skin, bark, hide, or even in the earth or mud. Small children had to read the picture instructions left them by their mother in the dust, and paintings on hides were often done by warriors to record their exploits. These were sometimes called "brag skins." It is such pictorial history that is reproduced on the pages of this book. While most of these works were done by Amos Bad Heart Buffalo, many were created by individuals wishing to preserve their own view of their people's history.

Amos Bad Heart Buffalo's drawing of himself as a cowboy, done Dec. 3, 1900. The inscription, translated by Helen Blish, reads, "Oglalas from White Clay district herding their cattle." The sketch at upper left is of a cattle ranch of that time, and the label above it reads, "Chenney River S. Dak. Squn Hamper Creek."

An Indian Horse Dance.

THE DAILY LIFE
OF THE PLAINS INDIANS

This painting depicts an Indian Horse Dance. This particular ceremony, held by the horse society, was recorded by Kills Two, and is undated. In this cult, thunder and lightning are important symbols, as the markings on both horses and men indicate.

Nomads and Hunters

The Plains Indian tribes were nomads, and moved their camps to follow the buffalo herds, or to find fresh pasture for their ponies. Each tribe had its traditional way of migrating, and the first two drawings on the following pages, by Amos Bad Heart Buffalo, show the main points of the Sioux style.

Amos's sketches depict a tribal migration. In the overall view, the four chiefs of the tribal council may be seen marching on foot, spearheading the column. On either side, the lieutenants ride their horses. They rode in groups in order to watch over the squaws and children who followed with the pony travois. The translation of the Lakota inscription by Helen Blish is: "The Teton Lakota—the traveling—whenever they are moving camp, the parties afoot go first. There are the men known as the body of council men, or Wakicunza. On each side of those that are afoot ride some on horseback. There are the dog soldiers or sergeants called Akicita; these watch over the people."

On the page following is a detail of this main scene. It shows how the wigwam ridge poles were lashed to the saddles to form the cradle which carried all the household equipment and the wigwam covers of buffalo hide.

To the Plains Indian, the buffalo was the source of all good things material and spiritual. The hides were for clothes, shoes, and wigwam walls; the meat was food; the sinews were for weapons and cord; the horns or hoofs were used for implements and adornment. No part was wasted. The buffalo entered into many aspects of their religious rituals as well, appearing as an important symbol again and again. The Indians' personal names were often a variation on the word "buffalo."

Three paintings of buffalo hunts follow Amos's migration sketches. The first, painted by Kills Two on canvas, shows in detail the equipment used by the Indians. The second was done by Shoshone Chief Washake on antelope skin in 1898 when he was almost 100 years old. The scene shows one animal being killed (top left) with a single arrow, one (below) needing two arrows, and a third getting away. The animal to the right (below the dark pink horse) fell and broke his neck. The painting is owned by C. A. Carter of Los Angeles, who was given it directly from Chief Washake. Finally, three sections of a painting on elk skin by the Shoshone, Katsikodi, are reproduced.

Lakota Oyate. Titon Ware.

tohanl ikdaka oyala. Wicasa maka
amanipi kena tokaheya maunpi
kena Waki kunza eWica Kijapi elpi
ito acuk sunk akan yanka maunpi
kena akicita piku hena elpi
Oyate ka Wita oWan Wiloyinkapi

Katsikodi's painting, reproduced on this and the preceding
two pages, bears an almost eerie resemblance to the well-known
cave paintings of the Bison at Altamira. In the sureness of its dash
and style, it is set apart from other, more painstaking Indian art of
the Plains. Here the usual crabbed fidelity of so many fine Indian
paintings is replaced by sweeping strokes that create a naturalness
beyond nature.

One example of the Indians' ability to make full use of every part of a buffalo may be found in the picture reproduced on the facing page. Here, a war party without squaws or kettles cooks a buffalo. The Lakota inscription as translated by Helen Blish identifies the place where the party is resting (upper right), describes the actions of butchering the buffalo, cooking with the paunch, heating the stones, and finally, the cooking of the meat. Frank Grouard gives a good description of this operation which fits this picture almost exactly.

"After making a big fire with the buffalo chips, the Indians put rocks in the fire. Next, they took the paunch out of a buffalo, and, after emptying it of its contents, turned it inside out and filled it with water. It must have held fifteen or twenty gallons. Then they took four bows, stuck them in the gravel, and fastened them together at the top, suspending the paunch between the bows. As soon as the stones were heated, they were put into the waterfilled paunch, and the same result was obtained as if the water had been placed in a tea kettle on top of the stove or over a fire. The stones were constantly changed, the meat was put into the boiling water and cooked."

In this picture the bows are replaced by forked sticks which are also used to pick up the heated stones, as can be seen on each side of the fire. The cooked meat, when taken out, was laid near the fire on branches and even leaves (lower right). This whole operation as drawn by Amos Bad Heart Buffalo and described by Grouard was the most self-contained possible. The animal not only provided the pot to cook the meat in (an instance of a real "flesh pot," or "potbelly") but his dung was the fuel to fire it all.

In the pictures reproduced on the following pages, two more activities revolving about the buffalo are shown. In the first, the participants in a ceremony are drawn with their costumes. The translation of the Lakota reads:

1. *Making (or imitating) buffalo*
2. *Making wounded*
3. *Making strange dogs (coyotes or wolves)*
4. *This is a place where the buffalo was killed*

In the second, the operation of tanning buffalo hides is pictured. The translation of the Lakota reads: "Handling the raw hides. There are ten doings connected with this."

All over the world the hunter gave way to the agriculturist long ago, but the Plains Indians lingered on as hunters into the industrial age. They were forced to abandon their traditional lifestyle only when the whites destroyed the buffalo, and that was less than 100 years ago.

Ozuye Oyuspa Najicla

Tasiga on Wohanpi

Pteizcoka Wapaltapi

Zuuga aśican. cega won śkes i pte wany "Opuki
he nigi kiúon Wohanpi Ptipi nainyan Kaś
pi śśa mini Okaś tan pin nainyan Ka té kin
Okuakapi can ipiga Ca lo śpangajpi

petayingan Oletipi gni kclos

Pela panikin

Ićázo k'ikóžu ta opi kóžu eċiyapi

Heyoka.

Sunkáto kaka kógu

Tatanka
Yeleohtehin
ee

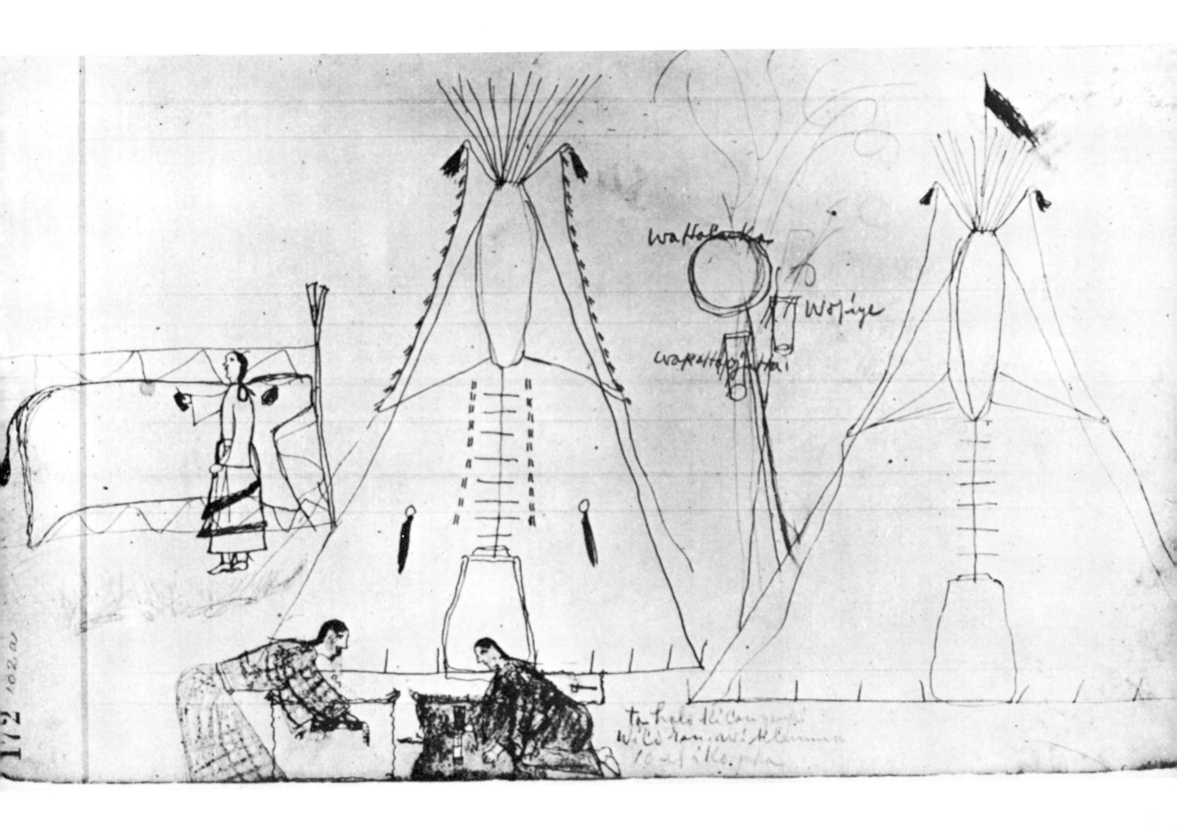

Indian Wars

The Plains Indians were warriors as well as nomads and hunters. A man's prowess on the battlefield was important in their society, and many Indian paintings were done in celebration of the exploits of particular individuals. One of the most famous warriors among the Plains Indians was the Sioux, Afraid-of-His-Horse (Tasenke Kokipapi), who is shown here in a painting by Kills Two. Afraid-of-His-Horse was a much feared warrior, and his name should be seen as the last four words in this sentence: "His enemies were even afraid of his horse." Other warriors had to make their own "brag skins"; Pretty Hawk, a Yanktomais Sioux, created the painting on skin reproduced on the page following in 1864 as part of his personal record of great exploits in his career. Taking many scalps was important to a warrior's reputation, but being known as a good horse thief was perhaps a finer thing. These paintings were hung in the lodges as we would place a wall-hanging.

The painting opposite that of Pretty Hawk is by Amos Bad Heart Buffalo, and depicts the return of a triumphant Sioux war party. According to Short Bull, who was in the party and appears as the last warrior on the left, the event took place in 1878. The artist was then a child of nine and could be one of the children seen in the background between the wigwams, standing with the squaws. His father, Bad Heart Bull the Elder, is leading the charge, with his fox-skin charm (battle protection) *wotawe* hanging over his left shoulder. The second man in the line is Black Deer (Tarca Sapa) with his personal charm, a flute decorated with a banner of feathers, which Short Bull says was intended to hang on a lance. There was no wood for a lance, so it was hung on the flute. Like Short Bull, he is riding a captured pinto pony. The inscription, translated by Helen Blish, reads, "It is generally the custom on the return from a successful war expedition for the returning warriors to charge at a run around the camp, firing guns as they go."

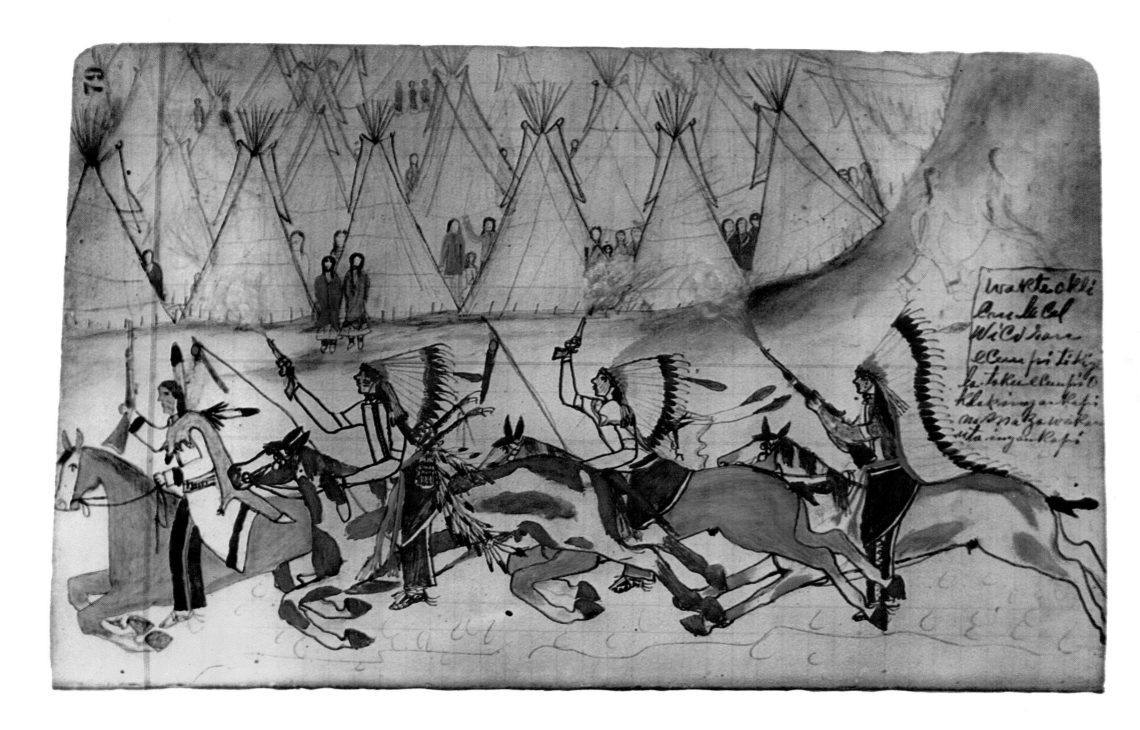

Pawnee and Sioux in battle
Zinťka Mato.

The painting on canvas by Kills Two reproduced above shows the killing of a Pawnee warrior by the Sioux lancer Dog Bear (Zinkta Mato). The Pawnees lived to the south of the Sioux and were their hereditary enemies. A mounted Sioux sabers a Pawnee bowman in this next painting by the same artist. The bowman was apparently a poor shot; his arrow can be seen at top right.

This painted buffalo skin from the Mandan tribe was brought back by Lewis and Clark in 1805. It is in the archaic style and shows a cavalry battle between the Minetaree and the allied forces of Sioux and Arikara. The painting on canvas by Kills Two has its origins later in Indian history. A Sioux is pictured attacking a Crow with his long knife, a weapon adopted by the Indians which was actually a U.S. Cavalry saber. This one may have been taken at the Battle at the Little Big Horn River.

The painting reproduced above is by Kills Two. Different artists drew their horses in quite varying ways. One school put in all the hoofs first, and built the drawing upwards in an architectural way. The next painting was done on canvas by the same artist and shows the warrior Red Walker and his companion fleeing from Crows. Red Walker has had a leg broken and his horse is wounded.

Love and Courtship

Amos Bad Heart Buffalo's drawing bears an inscription translated by Helen Blish as "Indian Love Flute." This Indian version of the Orpheus legend is best told in Helen Blish's own words. Her informant on this was He Dog.

"The central figure in the drawing is that of a man; he is robed in a decorated buffalo skin, his face is painted yellow with two red diagonal stripes on the cheek, he wears an eagle feather in his hair, and he plays a flute. This figure is framed by a circle, the right half of whose circumference is red, the left, yellow. The wavy blue line reaching from the oddly represented *sound,* issuing from the flute, to the yellow ring of the circle indicates that this man's music possessed spiritual powers not usually found in flute music. Behind the figure, just outside the circle, are eight women's heads; in front, outside the circle, are more.

"The explanation given is this: In the old days each man followed some special interest, usually war and the chase, of course. This man, however, followed the "elk activity," that is, his greatest interest was playing with the affections of women.

"He was player of the flute, the instrument of love, and elk medicine had made the call of this flute irrestistible to women throughout the whole circle of his world (therefore the circle about him). The eight heads outside the circle and behind him are like notches on a gun butt: they represent eight women who have already fallen victim to his charms. The heads before him represent victims yet to come.

"According to Dakota tradition, hundreds of years ago a man (not a Sioux or a Cheyenne) appeared in the land of the Dakotas, bringing the magic love flute. It is the belief of He Dog and Short Bull that this is the being represented in young Amos Bad Heart Buffalo's drawing.

"The red of the enclosing circle, they say, shows that this being was Indian, though no one knows to what tribe he belonged.

"The significance of the yellow of the circle if not known. This Being wore split deer-hoof rattles on his ankles as part of his equipment. Here He Dog adds this whimsical bit from his own experience: When they were camped on Cheyenne River, they used to hear a sound like that of deer hoofs rattling, and they thought it was this old Being walking."

kin Hanska natan Ki lakota kin
ya Cantipi Keyapi Akez Wanji la cantipi
Rce Woakiowi Ce yunkan Okiciyuspa
yle ou ou na keketu iye yapi ktasu le
ris Niciyuspe kin le (milala eciyapi)
spa najin kin le etipi Han Hepi etu
ken Wi Calakeya.

(milala) Wiina kinca eyaya
Han Hepis Ci nupa eu Wasna i na kinca
eyaye. na Hece na Han Hepi ta ke na
Waklu Kata Kiya eyayapi na Ogenpiapi
ki he hantu. na tun a Ki.

Courting among the Sioux was done with the man's blanket wrapped around the girl. Usually they eloped, as in this work by Amos Bad Heart Buffalo. This scene shows Milala (Pte San Yatapi) courting his wife on the left of her wigwam, and on the right, shows them eloping. This particular courting scene was chosen out of the many Amos did because of its relevance to the Battle at the Little Big Horn River. The translation of the Lakota reads:

1. A controversy arose among the Sioux. Some insisted that Custer charged on them the morning after the second night of their encampment on the Little Big Horn; others maintained that he came the first morning. Milala (Knife), whose correct name is King of the White Buffaloes (Pte San Yatapi), claims and proves that it was the morning after the second night, for on the first night he courted his wife and on the second she consented and eloped with him. He was not in the fight.
2. This shows Milala eloping with his bride toward Fort Laramie. Next morning they could hear the roar of battle north of them.

One of the love stories told by the Plains Indians revolves about the love of the Indian woman Me-o-tzi for General Custer. When Kate Bighead related her version of the Battle at the Little Big Horn River to Dr. Thomas Marquis, she made mention of this woman, her cousin. Her story may be pieced together as follows:

It was at Fort Sill that Me-o-tzi came to know the general. He was an important man in the eyes of her people then, for they had come there only after he promised peace to the chiefs of the Cheyenne. He was a familiar sight about the fort, a commanding figure marked by a large nose and long red hair; the Indian women considered him handsome. Me-o-tzi saw him often, and accompanied him regularly on expeditions that called for her aid as a tracker.

When Custer was transferred away from the Fort, Me-o-tzi remained behind. She was a popular young woman, and many Cheyennes would have married her; however, she remained faithful to the man she called her husband, insisting that he would some day return to her. Her story spread among her people, and its influence followed Custer to the Battle at the Little Big Horn seven years later. The Cheyenne women insist that it was they who first recognized Custer among the dead, and that it was for Me-o-tzi's sake that they protected his body from mutilation. Such respect did not comfort Me-o-tzi when she learned of the general's death. She mourned for him as an Indian woman mourns her husband, cutting off her hair and cutting her arms and legs. After seven years of waiting, she had lost Custer in a battle fought against her own people.

When Me-o-tzi did marry, she did not choose a Cheyenne. She married a white man by the name of Isaac, and bore him several children. Of her children, one did return to live with the Northern Cheyenne on Tongue River; Me-o-tzi herself died in January, 1921, in distant Oklahoma.

Joseph White Cow Bull was one of the young men who admired Me-o-tzi; his account of the Battle at the Little Big Horn River begins with his own story of himself and the Cheyenne girl.

JOSEPH WHITE COW BULL:
his account

The Shahiyela (*Cheyenne*) camp was farthest north. We Oglala were camped just southeast of them, with the Brule in a smaller circle next to us. Next were the Sans Arc, then the Miniconjou, the Blackfoot Sioux, and farthest south next to the river were the Hunkpapa. I was twenty-eight years old that summer.

While we were together in this village, I spent most of my time with the Shahiyela since I knew their tongue and their ways almost as well as my own. In all those years I had never taken a wife, although I had had many women. One woman I wanted was a pretty young Shahiyela named Monahseetah, or Me-o-tzi as I called her. She was in her middle twenties but had never married any man of her tribe. Some of my Shahiyela friends said she was from the southern branch of their tribe, just visiting up north, and they said no Shahiyela could marry her because she had a seven-year-old son born out of wedlock and that tribal law forbade her getting married. They said the boy's father had been a white soldier chief named Long Hair; he had killed her father, Chief Black Kettle, in a battle in the south (*Battle of the Washita*) eight winters before, they said, and captured her. He had told her he wanted to make her his second wife, and so he had her. But after a while his first wife, a white woman, found her out and made him let her go.

Yes, I saw him often around the

after a painting by David Humphreys Miller

Shahiyela camp. He was named Yellow Bird and he had light streaks in his hair. He was always with his mother in the daytime, so I would have to wait until night to try to talk to her alone. She knew I wanted to walk with her under a courting blanket and make her my wife. But she would only talk with me through the tepee cover and never came outside.

That morning many of the Oglalas were sleeping late. The night before, we held a scalp dance to celebrate the victory over Gray Fox (*General Crook*) on the Rosebud a week before. I woke up hungry and went to a nearby tepee to ask an old woman for food. As I ate, she said:

"Today attackers are coming."

"How do you know, Grandmother?" I asked her, but she would say nothing more about it.

After I finished eating I caught my best pony, an iron-gray gelding, and rode over to the Cheyenne camp circle. I looked all over for Me-o-tzi and finally saw her carrying firewood up from the river. The boy was with her, so I just smiled and said nothing. I rode on to visit with my Shahiyela friend Roan Bear. He was a Fox warrior, belonging to one of that tribe's soldier societies, and was on guard duty that morning. He was stationed by the Shahiyela medicine tepee in which the tribe kept their Sacred Buffalo Head . . . . We settled down to telling each other some of our brave deeds in the past. The morning went by quickly, for an Elk warrior named Bobtail Horse joined us to tell us stories about his chief, Dull Knife, who was not there that day.

The first we knew of any attack was after midday, when we saw dust and heard shooting way to the south near the Hunkpapa camp circle . . .

Just then an Oglala came riding into the circle at a gallop.

"Soldiers are coming!" he shouted in Sioux. "Many white men are attacking!"

I put this into a shout of Shahiyela words so they would know. I saw the Shahiyela chief, Two Moons, run into camp from the river, leading three or four horses. He hurried toward his tepee, yelling:

"Nutskaveho! White soldiers are coming! Everybody run for your horses!"

"Hay-ay! Hay-ay!" The Shahiyela warriors shouted their war cry, waiting in a big band for Two Moons to lead them into battle.

"Warriors, don't run away if the soldiers charge you," he told them. "Stand and fight them. Watch me. I'll stand even if I am sure to be killed!"

It was brave-up talk to make them strong in their fight. Two Moons led them out at a gallop . . .

"They're coming this way!" Bobtail Horse shouted. "Across the ford! We must stop them!"

We saw the soldiers in the coulee were getting closer and closer to the ford, so we trotted out to meet them. An old Shahiyela named Mad Wolf, riding a rack-of-bones horse, tried to stop us, saying:

"My sons, do not charge the soldiers. There are too many. Wait until our brothers come back to help!"

He rode along with us a way, whining about how such a small war party would have no chance against a whole army. Finally Bobtail Horse told him:

"Uncle, only Earth and the Heavens last long. If we four can stop the soldiers from capturing our camp, our lives will be well spent . . ."

The Sans Arc and Miniconjou camp circles were back from the

ford. We found a low ridge along here and slid off our ponies to take whatever cover we could find. For the first time I saw five Sioux warriors racing down the coulee ahead of the soldiers. They were coming fast and dodging bullets the soldiers were firing at them. Then Bobtail Horse pointed to that bluff beside the ford. On top were three Indians that looked like Crows from their hairstyle and dress. Bobtail Horse said:

"They are our enemies, guiding the soldiers here."

He fired his muzzleloader at them, then squatted behind the ridge to reload. I fired at them too, for I saw they were shooting at the five Sioux warriors, who were now splashing across the ford at a dead run. My rifle was a repeater, so I kept firing at the Crows until these Sioux were safely on our side of the river. They had no guns, just lances and bows and arrows. But they got off their ponies and joined us behind the ridge. Just then I saw a Shahiyela named White Shield, armed with bow and arrows, come riding downriver. He was alone, but we were glad to have another fighting man with us. That made ten of us to defend the ford.

I looked across the ford and saw that the soldiers had stopped at the edge of the river. I had never seen white soldiers before, so I remember thinking how pink and hairy they looked. One white man had little hairs on his face (a moustache) and was wearing a big hat and a buckskin jacket. He was riding a fine-looking big horse, a sorrel with a blazed face and four white stockings. On one side of him was a soldier carrying a flag and riding a gray horse, and on the other was a small man on a dark horse. This small man didn't look much like a white man to me, so I gave the man in the buckskin jacket my attention. He was looking straight at us across the river. Bobtail Horse told us all to stay hidden so this man couldn't see how few of us there really were.

The man in the buckskin jacket seemed to be the leader of these soldiers, for he shouted something and they all came charging at us across the ford. Bobtail Horse fired first, and I saw a soldier on a gray horse (not the flag carrier) fall out of his saddle into the water. The other soldiers were shooting at us now. The man who seemed to be the soldier chief was firing his heavy rifle fast. I aimed my repeater at him and fired. I saw him fall out of his saddle and hit the water.

Shooting that man stopped the soldiers from charging on. They all reined up their horses and gathered around where he had fallen. I fired again, aiming this time at the soldier with the flag. I saw him go down as another soldier grabbed the flag out of his hands. By this time the air was getting thick with gunsmoke and it was hard to see just what happened. The soldiers were firing again and again, so we were kept busy dodging bullets that kicked up dust all around.

From an interview conducted by David Humphreys Miller in 1938 and translated in his "Echoes of the Little Big Horn."

This scene painted by Silver Horn illustrates the legendary story of the Comanche chief and his wife who encountered a Ute warrior. The chief calls to his wife to spear the Ute, but she is in love at first sight with him, and turns her spear against her husband. However, he succeeds in throwing down the Ute, and she changes heart and cuts off the warrior's head. Later, the woman's brother kills her with arrows, as the penalty for her momentary treason.

INDIAN CEREMONIES

Some of the Indians who had to "sing for their supper" joined such touring shows as Buffalo Bill Cody's, but some gave shows on the reservation, which Amos Bad Heart Buffalo called "Greater Indian Shows." The one reproduced at the right was part of the "Give Away" ceremony. An Indian's prestige in the community had always been measured in direct proportion to how much he could give away. The ceremony went back to earliest times, and was a means of seeing that the poor and needy, such as the squaws with no husbands to hunt for their meat, were taken care of. After the white man's victory the ceremony kept on and was often performed on the Fourth of July (as the one shown, 1898). Another "Give Away" ceremony took place upon the death of an important person. As the Sioux saying goes, "Only those things not made less by division are to be passed on." However, this cermonial giving got out of hand, as these words of Amos Bad Heart Buffalo show (translated by Helen Blish):

> Someone had made himself poor helping the poor and needy (i.e. he has spared nothing). From this kind of Fourth of July celebration the people are getting poorer. Independence Day will keep on getting greater; it will be a thing to remember. But with misunderstanding we Indians celebrate and give away many useful articles unnecessarily. On that account the Indians will get poorer. And no one can be blamed but the tribe itself. If it could be that the people would be discreetly regulated, it would be all right, but there is no one to indicate the right limit in the give-away. For that reason, if this is kept up, the Indian will give away his last horse; he will go that far to satisfy the demands of a pleasure-seeking people.

Warrior parades, as recreated on the next two pages by Amos Bad Heart Buffalo, provided the audience with another means of measuring prestige. Each detail in his drawings gives a clue to the particular warrior society that the Indian belonged to. On the first page, the lead warrior beside the bow-lance holder wears the headgear of the Wicicka society. Amos Bad Heart Buffalo could draw horses from any view, as his rendering of the two charging front on (at the left) demonstrates.

Two drawings by Amos Bad Heart Buffalo depict the Grass Dance (Pejin Miknaka wacipi), meaning "grass tucked in the belt." In the first, all eight of the chosen dancers are "charging the dog" (left) in the dance's opening movement. The dog is a prairie dog and he is cooking in the food kettle (extreme left, his head peers out of the kettle). During this involved ceremony, small pieces of dog meat were served to distinguished guests on a pointed stick, the "dog fork." The most important guests were presented with whole dog heads.

The Indians tell many stories about the prairie dog and the coyote. One is a description of how the coyote catches the prairie dog during a rain. The coyote knows when it will rain, goes to where the prairie dog has its home, and destroys the platforms it builds to sit on when its burrow is flooded with rain. When it rains, the coyote grabs the prairie dog who is flushed out of its home. The coyote also catches the prairie dog by knowing that it peers out of its burrow until it sees the coyote charging. Then it will duck in until the coyote passes, and peer out again in the direction of the charge. For this reason, the coyote hunts in twos—the second close behind, in the shadow of the first.

The second drawing shows the Grass Dance of the Omaha Society given to commemorate one particular battle.

In this fight, the Indians drove off the soldiers under Col. J. J. Reynolds when they attacked and burned the Sioux-Cheyenne village on the Powder River, March 17, 1876. Most of the Indians involved in the Battle at the Little Big Horn River on June 25 thought that they were fighting this same army group (a part of Crook's command). They did not know that they were fighting Custer. During this ceremony, a special song was composed and sung in honor of Amos Bad Heart Buffalo's uncle, He Dog. The words are: He was their friend
They were his friends
Everyone hailed him
Even his own people

The following series of four drawings by Amos Bad Heart Buffalo were done during July 1898 and 1903 depicting the "Smoothing-the-Place-Dance." This was originally a part of the Sun Dance ritual, but became a preliminary movement to several other ceremonies. The first three drawings show warriors on the way to the dance. In the second, the fur charm worn by the fourth in line is the skin of an otter with a double row of small round mirrors set evenly along its length.

These go to Warrior Dancing

Another group goes to the dance in the third painting. They carry flags that show that this one was to be performed on the Fourth of July. The last drawing was made in 1898, and, translated by Helen Blish, the inscription reads, "This is the Smoothing-of-the-Place Dance." Warriors on foot surround the dance area. The green behind them represents the pineboughs that encircle and shade the dance ground. The medicine man, holding up a scalp stick, leads specially chosen warriors who ride horses. It is said they were chosen because they had rescued comrades under fire.

Iwankadnásto wociŋ́iƙel.

Four paintings on the Shoshone Sun Dance are reproduced on the following pages. The first, by Amos Bad Heart Buffalo, is an illustrated list of the ritual symbols involved in this, the most important of Indian ceremonies. Helen Blish translates the detailed inscriptions as follows:

(Center) *The sacred ground of Sun Dance (i.e., the altar)*
(Right)   *(1) The hole for the sacred pole is dug by a man of good habits.*
          (2) In the forks of the trees is placed a large pouch with a smaller pouch inside it containing the pemmican. Another pouch contains red paint. It is used to paint the sacred pole.
          (3) A short picket pin painted red is also included and hung with the other things in the fork of the pole.
          (4) An image of a man. An image of a buffalo.
(Left)   *(1) Red Flannel*
          (2) Pemmican pouch
          (3) Moccasin painted red
          (4) Branch of a tree painted with leaves
          (5) The prepared ground
          (6) Skull of a buffalo
          (7) Two pipes
          (8) Pole or stick painted blue

All sorts of rituals were observed at the Sun Dance festival. The young warriors were tested for courage by having hooks fastened first into their chests, and then onto the tree. Those given to sacred vision would cut themselves in order to fall into a trance that could bring on a vision of the future. At the Sun Dance before the Battle at the Little Big Horn River, Sitting Bull cut hundreds of wounds in his arms and legs, and finally saw a vision of white soldiers falling into the Indian camp. This, to Sitting Bull, promised a great victory soon to come.

The Kiowa variation of the Sun Dance ritual, painted on deerskin by Silver Horn, is reproduced on the next two pages. The first shows the erection of the Sun Dance lodge, and the dragging of trees to the center site of the Forked Tree. His second painting shows the three stages of the preparation of the Forked Tree, or Sun Dance Pole. A captive woman strikes and chops the tree marked by four bars with a hatchet, while the medicine man and his assistants chant and shake rattles (bottom right). Next the fallen tree is consecrated by the medicine man as being now the symbol of God, the Father Spirit (left). Finally, the tree is erect, decked in its ritual accoutrement, and surrounded by the ceremonial tepees (above left).

The last painting depicts the Shoshone Sun Dance, as painted on muslin by an unknown Shoshone. It is now in the C. A. Carter collection, in Los Angeles.

In the center is the Forked Tree, symbol of God the Father. A buffalo skin and a sheaf of sage are seen above it, and the colored streamer symbolizes the sun in the sky. In later times, this old ceremony took on some of the Christian symbolism, with the sage across the Forked Tree held to be vaguely cruciform, and the twelve poles said to represent the twelve apostles (there are only eight in this painting).

Amos Bad Heart Buffalo's painting of the Victory, or Scalp Dance. This is the Oglala Sioux version. It is the dance that the woman relatives of warriors lost in the Battle at the Little Big Horn River would have performed around the center pole, on which hangs a scalp, a hand, and a foot of the enemy. The men acting as drummers would normally be in a circle to the right. The inscription is, "Kills and comes back, this is the way the Tetons dance for it" (the *it* being the scalp).

THE BATTLE AT THE LITTLE BIG HORN RIVER

". . . this new battle was a turmoil of dust and warriors and soldiers, with bullets whining and arrows hissing all around. Sometimes a bugle would sound and the shouting would get louder. Some of the soldiers were firing pistols at close range. Our knives and war clubs flashed in the sun. I could hear bullets whiz past my ears. But I kept going and shouting, It's a good day to die! so that everyone who heard would know I was not afraid of being killed in battle."

—*Dewey Beard*

ON THE OUTSKIRTS OF THE BATTLE

Kate Bighead was one of the women who mourned the loss of their dead after the Battle at the Little Big Horn River; her young nephew was among the warriors killed. Singing "strongheart songs" for him, she circled the battlefield until she came across him, lying wounded nearby. He died that night.

Years later, she was to retell the story of the Battle she thus witnessed to Dr. Thomas B. Marquis, who had begun work as government doctor for the Cheyenne Indian Reservation at Lamedeer, Montana, in 1922. The following account is based on the version first interpreted by Dr. Marquis.

Kate Bighead had always enjoyed watching the battles between the soldiers and her people, the Cheyenne Indians; in the course of a long lifetime, she had witnessed quite a few. But the one battle which remained most vividly in her mind was the Great Battle at the Little Big Horn River, the final confrontation between General Custer and the Indians.

Although Little Big Horn was the most famous encounter, it was not the first meeting between the Cheyennes and Hi-es-tzie, or Long Hair, as the Cheyennes called General Custer because of his long red locks. Early in the winter of 1868, Long Hair and his Seventh Cavalry attacked the Indians in their camp by the Washita River. The snows were sprinkled with the blood of Chief Black Kettle and other Cheyennes that day, as many men, women, and children were killed by the white men. The soldiers burned all their teepees and destroyed all their belongings, leaving the survivors at the mercy of the Oklahoma winter.

The snows melted as they always did, giving way to spring. Long Hair and his soldiers returned once again in search of the Cheyennes, and found them camped further west near the Red River. But this time Long Hair joined the Cheyennes in smoking the peace pipe, and peace was promised. It was then that Custer was given the name of Hi-es-tzie, and then that those long red locks became a familiar sight to Kate Bighead.

After Hi-es-tzie made his promises, many of the Cheyennes in Kate's tribe went with him to Fort Sill. Kate joined them, and stayed at the fort for a while before going to live with the Northern Cheyennes on their "first" reservation; their "first" reservation, because when gold was discovered nearby, the white people came and the Indians were told to leave for another. Many did, but many refused, saying their next reservation would be taken away also if the white people again changed their minds. In any case, the government confiscated the guns and ponies of those who did live on the reservations; a policy that discouraged many of the young men and hunters from obeying the directive. All the Cheyennes and Sioux were supposed to be living on some reservation in Dakota, but many Indians ignored the orders and went their own way. Kate and her two brothers were among those who left for the open plains.

Although the Indians were thus forced to fragment themselves, the separate bands of Indians were ultimately to join together as one huge group just as the branches of a river always flow together again at some point. Kate's band of Cheyennes was attacked by white soldiers again in the winter of 1876. While only a few Indians were killed, all the teepees and belongings were burned and the ponies driven away. They were

forced to seek help from a tribe of Oglala Sioux led by Chief Crazy Horse.

The two tribes, the Cheyennes and the Oglala Sioux, traveled together for several days before joining Sitting Bull and the Hunkpapa Sioux. Anticipating further attempts by soldiers to force them back to the reservations, the three bands of Indians decided to remain together, to travel and hunt together throughout the spring and summer month, as one strong group rather than as three smaller and weaker groups.

As conditions on the reservations in Dakota became worse, more and more Indians migrated west, many joining the three tribes. Three more tribes, the Arrows All Gone Sioux, the Miniconjou Sioux, and the Blackfeet—fragmented offshoots of once large tribes—joined the Cheyennes, Oglalas, and Hunkpapa to form an army of Indians. Each tribe remained separate, retaining their own identities as six camps with six chiefs, but they all traveled and hunted as one, like separate fingers on a six-fingered hand. Kate said that there were more Indians than she had ever seen in her life at one time.

The six tribes lived peacefully for several months, hunting buffalo, curing the meat for the winter months, and tanning buffalo hides. The Indians moved westward slowly, and in the early summer of 1876 set up camp at Reno Creek near the Little Big Horn River. After just one night the first sign of trouble appeared and the peace was disturbed when soldiers were spotted by some hunters to the south of the camp. Some of the young men went off to fight them; when they returned the next day they carried the bodies of several dead warriors with them.

The entire group of Indians moved the next day to the point where Reno Creek joined the Little Big Horn. After several nights, the chiefs decided the six tribes should travel to the mouth of the river, stopping several times along the way. Some of the hunters had seen large herds of antelope there, and plenty of food could be provided for the winter.

Camp was set up at the first scheduled stop with plans to remain for one night. Kate remembered the camp well because of its happy mood, with everyone fishing, washing, and swimming in the river. But just shortly after noon that day, the peace was shattered as two boys ran into the camp warning of soldiers. And then, Kate said, the shooting could be heard, shooting that was not to end until hundreds of people were killed. All women and children left the water, most going to hide in the brush. The old men, weak in body but still strong in spirit, urged the young men on into battle and helped them put on their war paint and dress. Some of the women carried away teepees and their belongings; others just ran with their children and a handful of necessities. War ponies were brought into camp from the herds and the warriors mounted them and galloped away.

Kate found herself a pony and followed the warriors to watch the fighting as she often did; this time her nephew, Noisy Walking, was old enough to do battle and he expected her to watch and sing songs to give him courage. Kate crossed the river, immediately behind the warriors. The shooting was sporadic and changed in location as the fighting shifted and several small battles broke out. One group of soldiers was running on foot, chased by Indians on horses, but many more were on the other side of the river. Warriors were arriving from each of the six camps, hordes of them eager to fight. Most were equipped with bow and arrow, for few had guns, and fewer still had bullets. For the type of fighting they were engaged in, bows and arrows were better anyway, as Kate points out in her account. The soldiers had quickly positioned themselves along a ridge after dismounting from their horses, and it was then that the difference in weaponry began to have its effect. Each time a soldier shot his rifle, he would first have to lift his head to aim, thus exposing himself to the Indians. Then, the gun gave off a puff of smoke each time it was fired, showing the location of the shooter. The Indians who used guns themselves had the same problems, but the Indians with arrows could shoot them without betraying their position in any way. In addition, by sending the arrows flying upward in the direction of the soldiers, the arrows would arc down toward their targets. The soldiers could not do this with their guns, and they would be hit by the great numbers of arrows falling in waves despite their hidden position.

Kate rode around the outer fringes of the fighting, staying out of range of the bullets as she searched for Noisy Walking. In this way, she could see everything that was happening. More and more Indians and soldiers were getting off their horses, preferring to hide or crawl along the ground. A man who remained on a horse was an easy target, and with all the shooting and screaming, most horses would not stay still to allow their riders to take good aim.

The ridge by the river became a definite focal point as bands of warriors moved toward the waiting soldiers. Hundreds of Indians had begun to crawl toward them along the crevices and gullies. At this stage, the fighting was slow and few were killed as both sides remained hidden. But some impatient soldiers soon mounted an attack off the ridge, galloping on their horses toward a group of Cheyennes and Oglalas. The Indians scattered to safety before the soldiers reached them, and the white men dismounted again to hide along a second ridge.

But the strength of the forces of the six tribes was too great for the soldiers, as dozens of warriors, both Cheyenne and Oglala Sioux, trickled back until there were hundreds surrounding this second ridge. One of the bravest Cheyenne warriors, Chief Lame White Man, was leading them. By Kate's estimation, there were almost twenty Indians to each soldier on the ridge. It was at this point that Kate first saw one of the soldiers point his pistol at his head and pull the trigger. Only too well aware of their situation, others imitated his example, shooting sometimes themselves, sometimes each other. The soldiers' horses were startled and broke loose, running away toward the river. Lame White Man finally called the warriors to attack. Fascinated, they hesitated an instant to watch this mass suicide, and then rushed toward the ridge. When they reached the soldiers, all of them were already dead.

As Kate continued her search for her nephew, she saw one soldier sitting all alone in a spot where the fighting had stopped. The man was frightened and confused, unaware of what was going on around him. Three Sioux crept up on him, grabbing and laying him out on the ground. As two of the warriors held him down, the third slowly cut off his head.

Indians were already searching among the corpses of the soldiers, collecting guns and ammunition. The women and old men rounded up the horses which had broken loose from the soldiers. Elsewhere the fighting continued. At the ridge where the soldiers had first situated themselves, the Indians finally attacked. Again, the soldiers' horses were frightened off, and when the Indians reached the top of the ridge, most of the white men were already dead. They had all killed themselves or each other in panic, just as the soldiers on the other ridge had. The only thing remaining for the Indians to do was pick up the abandoned guns and ammunition. As the warriors walked among the white men, they cut off the legs or feet or arms of many of the bodies. Some of the soldiers were still living, having only been wounded; but they were quickly killed and parts of their bodies were also severed.

Only a few soldiers were still alive and able to fight at this point, and they joined forces at the west end of the ridge. The warriors surrounded them, hundreds of Indians for each white man. The soldiers were terrified, for all around them a seemingly infinite number of Indian heads would suddenly rise from a clump of grass or from behind a rock, but only for a second, as they quickly disappeared out of sight again before a rifle could take aim. Frequently a warrior who had crept close enough would dash out to try to strike a deathblow at one of the remaining soldiers.

A great number of old men and young boys had gathered on the surrounding hills to watch the last traces of fighting. The old ones shouted instructions and words of caution, while the young ones, if they dared, rushed forward trying to gain the honor of a deathblow. As a result one Sioux boy was killed by a soldier bullet. The tense waiting soon brought silence, and the shooting stopped. The Indians thought all of the soldiers had been killed, and rushed toward the ridge to complete the battle with their rituals.

But seven soldiers were still alive; they rushed out from behind their horses and started running. Immediately hundreds of warriors started pursuing them. At the same time, hundreds of Indian boys descended upon the dead soldiers, eager to strike blows on the dead bodies of the enemy, thought to be a brave thing for an Indian boy to do. Kate could not see what happened to the seven soldiers because of all the dust raised by the Indians and their ponies, but later she heard the soldiers had killed themselves before the warriors reached them.

Kate rode away and moved slowly between the Indians and the dead soldiers, still searching for her nephew. She met a Cheyenne who told her that Noisy Walking had been shot and stabbed, and was resting down in the gulch toward the river. Kate went to him and stayed with him while a friend went to find his mother. Noisy Walking did not live long; he died that night. He was one of the few Indians to be killed—only half a dozen Cheyennes and two dozen Sioux lost their lives. The Indians said this was because of the Everywhere Spirit, who had caused the white men to go mad and kill themselves, thus saving many Indian lives from the guns of the soldiers. They said this madness was the Everywhere Spirit's way of punishing the white men for attacking a peaceful Indian camp.

The fighting had finally ended, but there was much work left to do. Some of the women brought in wooden sledges pulled by ponies to carry the dead and wounded Indians away. The women who had lost their men cried, and beat and cut the bodies of the dead soldiers in a ritual of revenge and mourning. Other Indians hunted through the dead bodies, pulling off boots and clothing, taking guns and ammunition, gathering horses and saddles.

The next afternoon, on the day after the battle, the dead were honored. According to their respective tribal customs, the Cheyennes were buried while some of the Sioux dead were placed in teepees, arranged as in a living camp. Scaffolds were built outside the camps upon which the other Sioux dead were placed. Since it was tradition to leave a camp when any of its inhabitants died, the chiefs chose new sites further down the river. The lodges and teepees were dismantled and preparations were made to continue the trip to the mouth of the Little Big Horn.

The six tribes left their camps in the valley where the Reno Creek joined the Little Big Horn River, leaving the scene of the Great Battle behind them. But they talked of the fighting for days afterward, and many stories were woven from the deeds done that day. Kate heard that the Cheyenne warriors had been considered the most important Indian fighters at the battle, for their camp had been located at the end of the group of six camps. It was there that the soldiers first attacked. The Cheyennes were helped for the most part by the Oglalas, their first traveling companions.

As the tribes traveled down the river, while memories of the fighting were barely a day old, some of the warriors rode back up the valley to fight the first group of soldiers they had encountered in their first Reno Creek camp. They fought there for another day and a half before they returned with word that more soldiers were coming toward the Little Big Horn area. The chiefs decided there had already been too much fighting, and hastened their trek down the Little Big Horn.

As they traveled along the river, the Indians made sixteen stops, making camp for one night only at each stop. The six tribes stayed together for the entire trip, but when they reached the junction of the Little Big Horn and the Powder River, they parted to go their separate ways. Kate and the Cheyennes continued to the mouth of the Powder River where they made camp. It was only after they had lived there for several months that they first learned that the leader of the soldiers at the Great Battle at Little Big Horn had been Hi-es-tzie, and that he had been killed there along with all his men.

The Cheyennes' quiet existence at the Powder River did not last long. When winter arrived, it brought with it more soldiers and more fighting and killing, just as winter had brought so often in the past. The Cheyenne lodges and teepees were destroyed, and with them, the hides and meat which they had saved through a summer's worth of hunting. In January of 1877 the soldiers attacked again, taking three women and several children hostage. One of the captured women, after a day of captivity, relayed a message back to the Cheyenne camp, saying the soldiers were great in number. But she said that she and her companions had been well treated, and urged the Cheyennes to surrender and go with the soldiers to the reservation. The Cheyennes did not heed her words, and instead moved back into the Little Big Horn valley for the rest of the winter.

In the spring the white men sent one of the captured women to find the Cheyennes in the Big Horn valley. When she did, she again urged the Cheyennes to go with the soldiers, and said the white men promised that the Indians would be well taken care of. She repeated her claim that she and the other captives had been well treated. Many of the Cheyennes were persuaded by the woman's arguments to go back to the white men, and they returned with her. After some time another group, including Kate Bighead and her brother, followed as well.

Thus the Cheyenne tribe was completely divided and scattered.

Some were still back in Dakota, others were traveling and hunting in small bands, refusing to go to a reservation. Many, including Kate, were placed in Oklahoma. While the Cheyenne tribe as a whole no longer existed, memories of the final confrontation between Hi-es-tzie and the Indians at Little Big Horn remained and stories still were told, as they would be for years to come. Two of the Cheyenne women in Kate's camp in Oklahoma said they had seen Hi-es-tzie lying dead on the battlefield at Little Big Horn, his long, wavy red hair covered with dust. They said that because of his special status, because the Cheyennes remembered the years they had lived with him at Fort Sill, they had accorded him special treatment. Instead of cutting off an entire arm or leg as the Indians did to the other dead soldiers, they cut off only one joint of one finger. They then pierced his eardrums with an awl, saying his hearing needed improvement; they remembered the time Hi-es-tzie had smoked the peace pipe with their chiefs. It seemed he had not heard the promises of peace he himself had made, nor the warning of the Cheyenne chiefs: they had told him that the Everywhere Spirit would kill him if he broke the peace.

This account is based on "She Watched Custer's Last Battle," text drawn from a 1927 interview conducted by Dr. Thomas B. Marquis and most recently published in his *Custer on the Little Bighorn*.

The main chieftains involved in the Battle at the Little Big Horn River portrayed (above) by Amos Bad Heart Buffalo. Although the note translates as "one of the leaders," there are clearly two. I believe the scene shows the two leaders exhorting their men to fight and win. On the facing page, Amos portrays the battle's leaders in a symbolic confrontation. The translation reads, "Long Hair came with a challenge." The names of General Custer, Crazy Horse, and Sitting Bull are written in English.

"Sitting Bull wailed aloud, offering a pipe as he prayed: 'Wakantanka, hear me and pity me! I offer you this pipe in the name of my people. Save them. We want to live! Guard my people against all danger and misfortune. Take pity on us!'"

—Henry Oscar One Bull

HENRY OSCAR ONE BULL: his account

It was the time when ponies are fat. During a sun dance we held on Rosebud Creek ten days earlier, my uncle, Sitting Bull, had offered a hundred pieces of his flesh to Wakantanka (*Great Holy Spirit*) and had been granted a vision of white soldiers without ears falling upside-down into camp. He told me that this vision was a promise of a great victory yet to come. Three days later we beat Gray Fox (*General George Crook*) in a fight on the Rosebud. But my uncle said an even greater victory was coming.

The night before the fight with Long Hair, Sitting Bull went out to the ridge where the monument now stands. He sang a thunder song, then prayed for knowledge of things to come. As he repeated for me later, he wailed aloud, offering a filled pipe as he prayed:

"Wakantanka, hear me and pity me! I offer you this pipe in the name of my people. Save them. We want to live! Guard my people against all danger and misfortune. Take pity on us!"

Then he stuck slender wands in the ground to which he tied tiny buckskin bags of tobacco and willow bark. Next day Long Hair's horse soldiers would knock them all down, but that night my uncle knew that Wakantanka had heard his prayer. Before sunup an old woman died in the Hunkpapa camp. She was the wife of Sitting Bull's uncle, Four Horns. As Sitting Bull later told me, the death of such an important woman made him wonder if the promised victory might not come that very day.

I was twenty-three that summer and had been a warrior a long time. Another Hunkpapa named Gray Eagle and I were Sitting Bull's special bodyguards. It was our duty to watch him and see that he had protection. I also had the duty of seeing that his orders were carried out by others and to look after his property. That morning I took the family horses to the river.

At midday I went back to the pony herd and drove the horses to the river for the noon watering. Just then I heard shooting near the Hunkpapa camp circle. I knew our camp soldiers (police) did not allow offhand firing. So I recognized the shots as a warning of some kind of danger. I quickly caught my best pony and turned the other stock loose, knowing they would head back to camp as soon as the hobbles were off. Not far away I saw dust rising and heard iron-shod hoofs pounding against loose rocks. I raced back to the tepee I shared with my uncle.

The Hunkpapa camp was in an uproar. Warriors were rushing around to catch their ponies. Women were screaming and children were crying and old men were shouting advice as loud as they could. Then the women and children began to run off to the west, not taking the time to strike their tepees or to carry off belongings.

I reached the tepee ahead of my uncle. I grabbed my old muzzleloader and quickly checked it. Just then Sitting Bull entered the tepee and took the old rifle out of my hands. He handed me a stone-headed war club, then took his own rawhide shield out of its buckskin case and hung it over my shoulder. This shield was both for protection and to be used as a badge of the chief's authority.

"You will take my place and go out and meet the soldiers that are attacking us," he ordered. "Parley with them, if you can. If they are willing, tell them I will talk peace with them."

Sitting Bull was buckling on his cartridge belt as we hurried outside. His deaf-mute adopted son came running up with the chief's black stallion. Another bodyguard, named Iron Elk, handed my uncle a Winchester carbine and a revolver and held the stallion's jaw rope. Sitting Bull jumped on the stallion's bare back and galloped off to look for his old mother and get her to safety. Many young warriors gathered around me. I raised my uncle's shield high so they all could see it. Then I led them out to meet the soldiers.

The soldiers were mixed up. Some got off their horses and began firing again as we rode in. Others stayed mounted. Two soldiers couldn't hold their horses in all the excitement. The horses bolted, carrying their riders right into our warriors. These soldiers didn't last long!

Then the soldier chief shouted something, and all the soldiers did a strange thing. They all got off their horses, except for every fourth man who held the horses for the other three. Then they ran on foot trying to get into the timber along the river. I raised my uncle's shield again and led another charge to chase them. They were turning around to shoot at us, but we rode right into them, chasing them into the river. We killed many on the river bank and in the water.

I rode up behind one soldier and knocked him over with my war club. Then I slid off my pony and held the soldier's head under water until he was dead. I killed two more soldiers in the water.

A Hunkpapa warrior named Good Bear Boy was riding alongside me and was suddenly shot off his horse. Black Moon fell about the same time. He was dead, but Good Bear Boy was only wounded. I ordered a warrior named Looking Elk to rescue him, but Looking Elk didn't hear me. Good Bear Boy tried to crawl back from the river. I saw many soldiers struggle across the river and climb out on the far

61

bank. They ran to a high butte (*now called Reno Hill*) and from there they kept shooting at us. Some of them dug holes (*trenches*) in the ground and got into these holes or behind their saddles so we couldn't hit them. I ordered warriors to surround the butte so the soldiers couldn't get away. I wanted to starve them out. A Lakota told me later that the warriors kept those soldiers there all night. Finally, the soldiers began to get crazy for water. The Lakotas (*Teton Sioux*) wouldn't let the soldiers go to the river to drink or get water to take back up to their holes in the ground. Two or three of them tried to crawl down to the river, but our warriors shot them.

Bullets were flying all around, but I saw that Good Bear Boy wasn't able to crawl back to camp. He was shot through both thighs and bleeding heavily. So I jumped off my pony long enough to help Good Bear Boy climb on, then I leaped up behind him. I heard my pony scream. A bullet had struck his hindquarters. I took Good Bear Boy back to camp and saw that his friends took care of him. As I left him, I saw three soldiers running on foot toward the river. They had gotten away from us earlier in the fight. I charged after them, and they ran very fast. I wanted to ride them down, but just then I heard my uncle's voice.

"O, come back, my son!" he shouted.

Sitting Bull had seen the blood of Good Bear Boy and my pony all over my legs and thought I was wounded. Then he said: "Let them go! Let them live to tell the truth about this fight!"

I obeyed. We let the three soldiers escape. My uncle looked worried.

"Nephew, you are wounded. Go to the women and have your wounds treated."

So I laughed, saying I wasn't wounded and telling him about Good Bear Boy.

"You have done well. You put up a good fight. Now go help defend the women and children and old ones. More soldiers may come."

I did as he ordered and joined our people west of the camp. Soon after I reached them, I saw more dust across the river. A second band of soldiers was riding down a coulee toward the ford by the Miniconjou camp circle. Another alarm went up. I saw a handful of warriors racing to the ford to meet them. Then more warriors left the soldiers surrounded on the butte and galloped over to head off this second attack. They chased these new soldiers out of the coulee and up onto a long ridge. More of our warriors, mostly Oglalas and Cheyennes, were waiting for these soldiers at the end of the ridge and caught them in a trap. They were all wiped out in a short time. My brother White Bull later said the leader of the second band of soldiers was Long Hair Custer. White Bull was fighting the soldiers on the ridge and he can tell you about that part of the battle.

"Henala! Enough!" my uncle shouted. "Those soldiers are trying to live, so let them live. Let them go. If we kill all of them, a bigger army will march against us."

From an interview conducted by David Humphreys Miller in 1938 and translated in his "Echoes of the Little Big Horn."

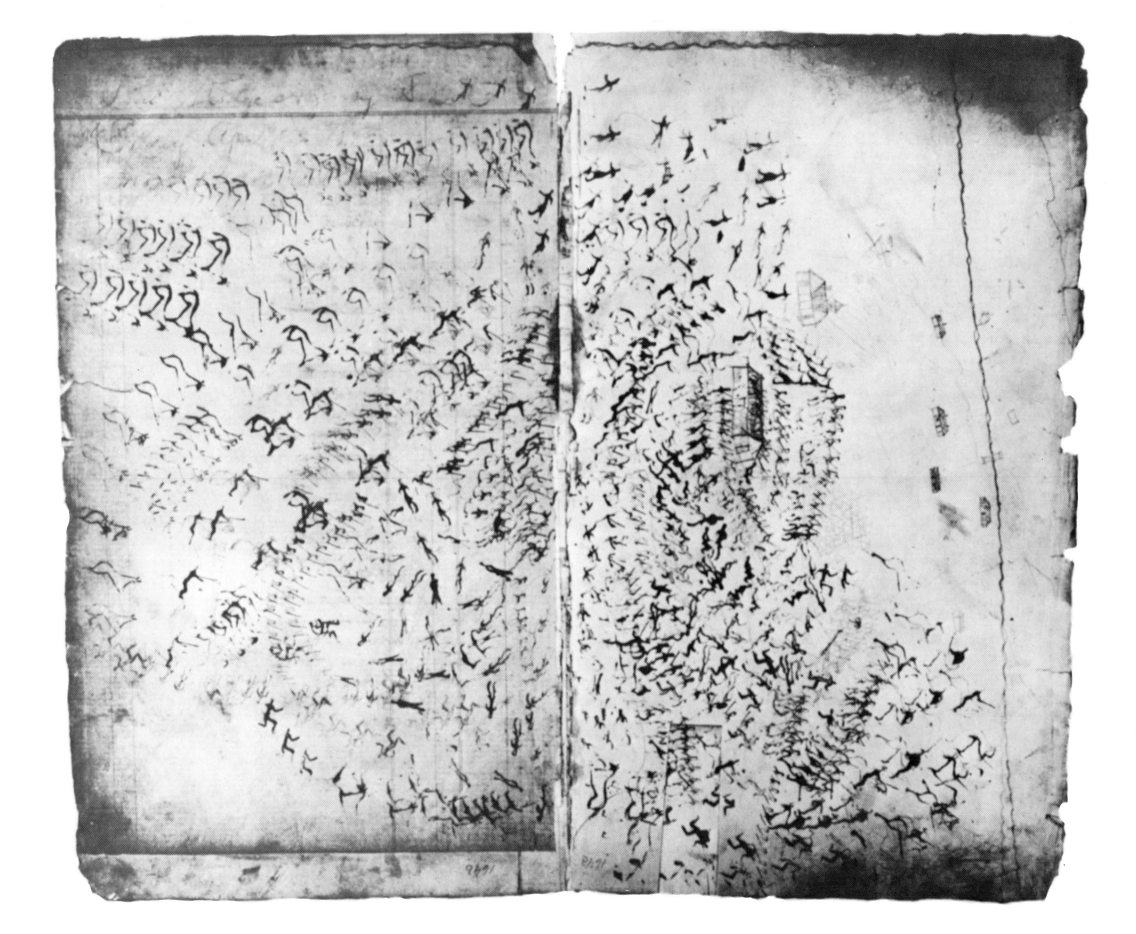

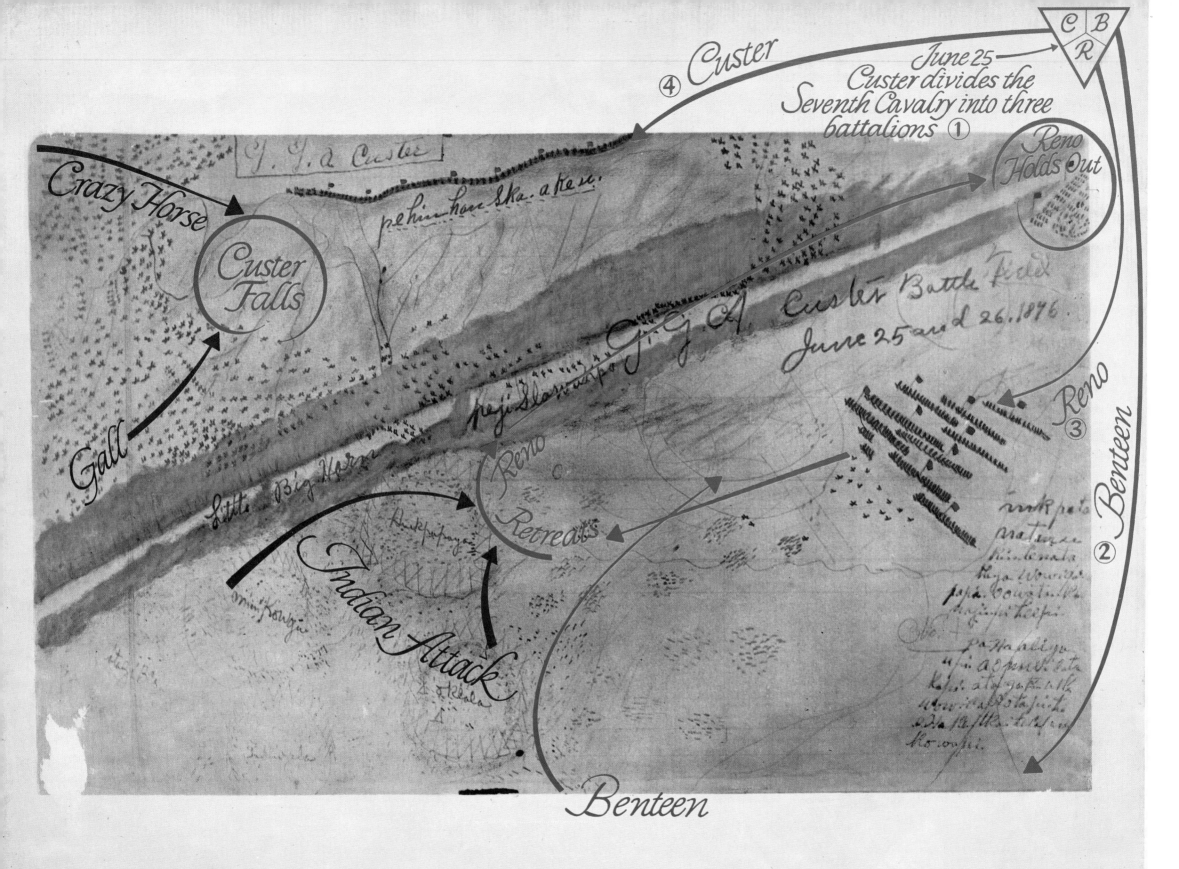

Custer

④ Custer

June 25
Custer divides the
Seventh Cavalry into three
battalions ①

Crazy Horse

Custer
Falls

Reno
Holds Out

G. G. A. Custer

pehin hau Ska. a keru.

Gall

G. G. A. Custer Battle Field
June 25 and 26. 1876.

Little Big Horn

Reno

Retreats

Reno
③

Benteen

Indian Attack

② Benteen

Benteen

64

I have attempted, with these notes drawn on and around Amos Bad Heart Buffalo's battle map, to explain the battle in four steps: 1-2-3-4 (in green).

1. Custer divides the Seventh Cavalry into three battalions.
2. Benteen to ride southeast to cut off any Indian escape in that direction.
3. Reno to attack the village frontally
4. His own group to ride across the ridge above the village and supposedly attack it from the rear.

Custer rode along the ridge, and was surrounded by Gall's and Crazy Horse's men. He was wiped out by about 5 o'clock on June 25th. Reno advanced to the village encampment, but was stopped, and sought cover in some trees. He was forced to move back, and there again had to retreat. He crossed the river and formed a defense on a bluff above it, where he was joined by Benteen and the mule packtrain. The Custer group was wiped out while Reno was retreating and grouping his forces. He was relieved two days later by General Terry.

This topographical sketch-map of the Battle at the Little Big Horn River by Amos Bad Heart Buffalo was accompanied by these words:

"In Montana. When Long Hair came charging on us, all of his men were killed. This is they (*referring to the ensuing drawings*). The Indian nation did not wish to fight; it is always they (*the whites*) that start shooting first and the Indian who starts last.

Along this stream (*outlined in pencil*) is the head of the Greasy Grass. They came in this fashion, all abreast. This is they who started shooting first and surprised the Indian tribes. All those who pretended to be men got their horses and got ready and met them with a shout and charged. The battle followed. In the first battle (*Reno's first charge*) perhaps ten got away. In another battle (*the fight with Custer's command*) all of those who came along the ridge were killed. Long Hair was with them."

Amos Bad Heart Buffalo's information would have come from the various Indian participants of the battle, particularly from his father, Bad Heart Bull the Elder, and from He Dog. Both were prominent warriors and fought in the thick of the battle.

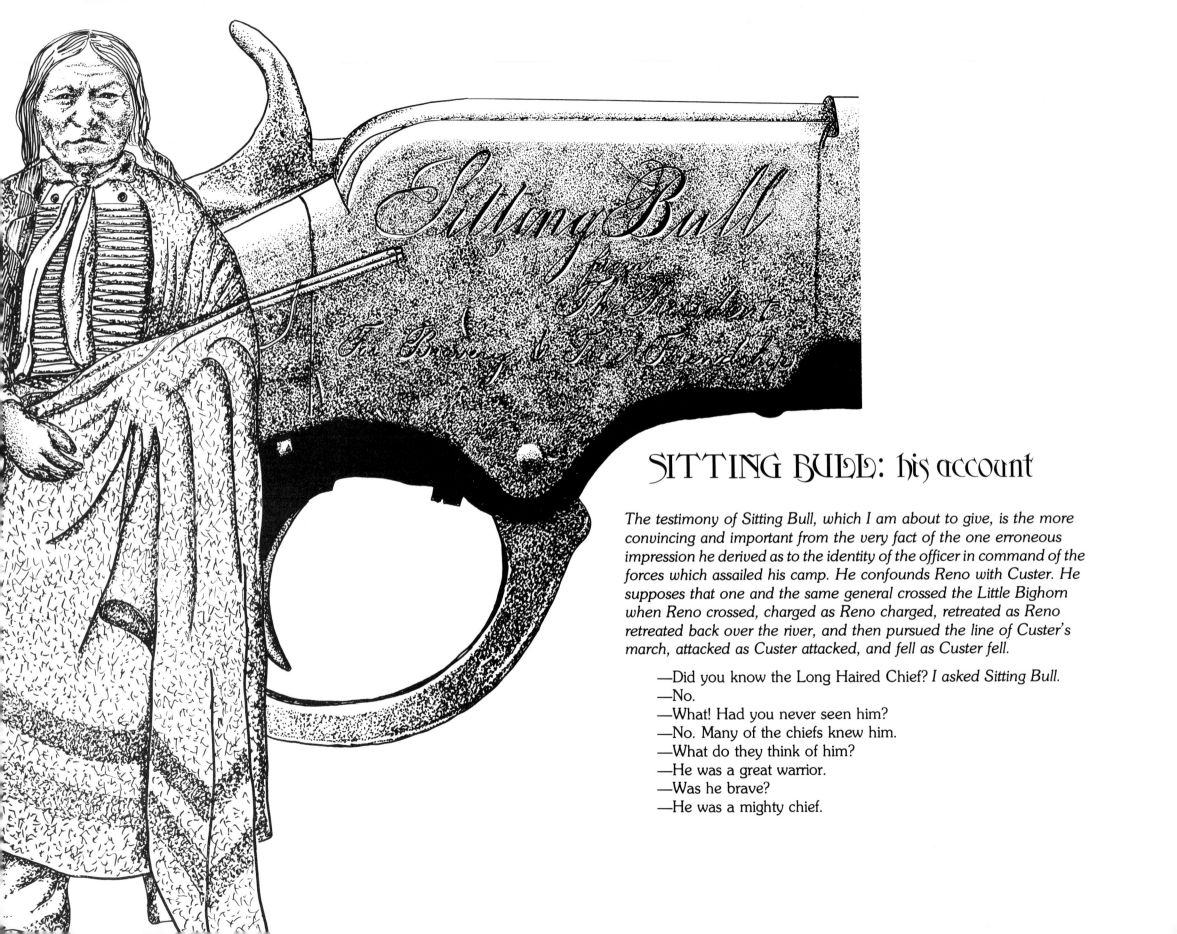

SITTING BULL: his account

The testimony of Sitting Bull, which I am about to give, is the more convincing and important from the very fact of the one erroneous impression he derived as to the identity of the officer in command of the forces which assailed his camp. He confounds Reno with Custer. He supposes that one and the same general crossed the Little Bighorn when Reno crossed, charged as Reno charged, retreated as Reno retreated back over the river, and then pursued the line of Custer's march, attacked as Custer attacked, and fell as Custer fell.

—Did you know the Long Haired Chief? *I asked Sitting Bull.*
—No.
—What! Had you never seen him?
—No. Many of the chiefs knew him.
—What do they think of him?
—He was a great warrior.
—Was he brave?
—He was a mighty chief.

—Now, tell me. Here is something that I wish to know. Big lies are told about the fight in which the Long Haired Chief was killed. He was my friend. No one has come back to tell the truth about him, or about that fight. You were there; you know. Your chiefs know. I want to hear something that forked tongues do not tell—the truth.

—It is well.

Here I drew forth a map of the battle field and spread it out across Sitting Bull's knees, and explained to him the names and situations as represented on it, and he smiled.

—We thought we were whipped, *he said.*

—Ah! Did you think the soldiers were too many for you?

—Not at first; but by-and-by, yes. Afterwards, no.

—Tell me about the battle. Where was the Indian camp first attacked?

—Here (*pointing to Reno's crossing on the map*).

—About what time in the day was that?

—It was some two hours past the time when the sun is in the centre of the sky.

—What white chief was it who came over there against your warriors?

—The Long Hair.

—Are you sure?

—The Long Hair commanded.

—But you did not see him?

—I have said that I never saw him.

—Did any of the chiefs see him?

—Not here, but there, *he said, pointing to the place where Custer*

charged and was repulsed, on the north bank to the Little Bighorn.

—Why do you think it was the Long Hair who crossed first and charged you here at the right side of the map?

—A chief leads his warriors.

—Was there a good fight here, on the right side of the map? Explain it to me.

—It was so, *said Sitting Bull, raising his hands.* I was lying in my lodge. Some young men ran in to me and said: The Long Hair is in the camp. Get up. They are firing in the camp. I said, all right, and jumped up and stepped out of my lodge.

—Where was your lodge?

—Here, with my people, *answered Sitting Bull, pointing to the group of Hunkpapa lodges designated as "abandoned lodges" on the map.*

—So the first attack was made, then, on the right side of the map, and upon the lodges of the Hunkpapas?

—Yes.

—Here the lodges are said to have been deserted?

—The old men, the squaws and the children were hurried away.

—Toward the other end of the camp?

—Yes. Some of the Miniconjou women and children also left their lodges when the attack began.

—Did you retreat at first?

—Do you mean the warriors?

—Yes, the fighting men.

—Oh, we fell back, but it was not what warriors call a retreat; it was to gain time. It was the Long Hair who retreated. My people fought him here in the brush (*designating the timber behind which the Indians pressed Reno*) and he fell back across here (*placing his finger on the line of Reno's retreat to the northern bluffs*).

—So you think that was the Long Hair whom your people fought in that timber and who fell back afterwards to those heights?

—Of course.

—What occurred afterward? Was there any heavy fighting after the retreat of the soldiers to the bluffs?

—Not then; not there.

—Where, then?

—Why, down here; *and Sitting Bull indicated with his finger the place where Custer approached and touched the river. That, said he,* was where the big fight was fought a little later. After the Long Hair was driven back to the bluffs he took this road (*tracing with his finger the line of Custer's march on the map*), and went down to see if he could not beat us there.

Here the reader should pause to discern the extent of Sitting Bull's error, and to anticipate what will presently appear to be Reno's misconception or mistake. Sitting Bull, not identifying Reno in the whole of this engagement, makes it seem that it was Custer who attacked, when Reno attacked in the first place, and afterward moved down to resume the assault from a new position. He thus involuntarily testifies to the fact that Reno's assault was a brief, ineffectual one before his retreat to the bluffs, and that Reno, after his retreat, ceased on the bluffs from aggressive fighting.

—When the fight commenced here, *I asked, pointing to the spot where Custer advanced behind the Little Big Horn,* what happened?

—Hell!

—You mean, I suppose, a fierce battle?

—I mean a thousand devils.

—The village by this time was thoroughly aroused?

—The squaws were like flying birds; the bullets were like humming bees.

—You say that when the first attack was made off here on the right of the map, the old men and squaws and children ran down the valley toward the left. What did they do when this second attack came from up here toward the left?

—They ran back to the right, here and there, *answered Sitting Bull, placing his swarthy fingers on the words "Abandoned Lodges."*

—And where did the warriors run?

—They ran to the fight—the big fight.

—So that in the afternoon, after the first fight, on the right-hand side of the map, was over, and after the big fight on the left-hand side began, you say the squaws and children all returned to the right-hand side, and that the warriors, the fighting men of all the Indian camps, ran to the place where the big fight was going on?

—Yes.

—Why was that? Were not some of the warriors left in front of these intrenchments on the bluffs, near the right side of the map? Did you not think it necessary,—did not your war chiefs think it necessary,—to keep some of your young men there to fight the troops who had retreated to these intrenchments?

—No.

—Why?

—You have forgotten.

—How?

—You forget that only a few soldiers were left by the Long Hair on those bluffs. He took the main body of his soldiers with him to make the big fight down here on the left.

—So there were no soldiers to make a fight left in the intrenchments on the right-hand bluff.

—I have spoken. It is enough. The squaws could deal with them. There were none but squaws and papooses in front of them that afternoon.

This startling assertion of Sitting Bull involves the most terrible charge which has been brought against Reno. It amounts to an assertion that Reno, having made his assault, been beaten and retreated, stayed there on the bluffs without renewing the attack for which General Custer, who had by this time come down with his horsemen on the rear of the Sioux camp from the north, vainly awaited—how hopelessly!

—Well, then, *I inquired of Sitting Bull,* did the cavalry, who came down and made the big fight, fight?

Again Sitting Bull smiled.

—They fought. Many young men are missing from our lodges. But is there an American squaw who has her husband left? Were there any Americans left to tell the story of that day?

—No.

—How did they come on to the attack?

—I have heard that there are trees which tremble.

—Do you mean the trees with trembling leaves?

—Yes.

—They call them in some parts of the Western country Quaking Asps; in the eastern part of the country they call them Silver Aspens.

—Hah? A great white chief, whom I met once, spoke these words, "Silver Aspens," trees that shake; these were the Long Hair's soldiers.

—You do not mean that they trembled before your people, because they were afraid?

—They were brave men. They were tired. They were too tired.

—How did they act? How did they behave themselves?

At this Sitting Bull again arose. I also arose from my seat, as did the other persons in the room, except the stenographer.

—Your people, *said Sitting Bull, extending his right hand,* were killed. I tell no lies about dead men. These men who came with the Long Hair were as good men as ever fought. When they rode up their horses were tired and they were tired. When they got off from their horses they could not stand firmly on their feet. They swayed to and fro—so many young men have told me—like the limbs of cypresses in a great wind. Some of them staggered under the weight of their guns. But they began to fight at once; but by this time, as I have said, our camps were aroused, and there were plenty of warriors to meet them. They fired with needle guns. We replied with magazine guns—repeating rifles. It was so (*and here Sitting Bull illustrated by patting his palms together with the rapidity of a fusillade*). Our young men rained lead across the river and drove the white braves back.

—And then?

—And then they rushed across themselves.

—And then?

—And then they found that they had a good deal to do.

—Was there at that time some doubt about the issue of the battle, whether you would whip the Long Hair or not?

—There was so much doubt about it that I started down there (*here again, pointing to the map*) to tell the squaws to pack up the lodges and get ready to move away.

—You were on that expedition, then, after the big fight had fairly begun?

—Yes.

—You did not personally witness the rest of the big fight? You were not engaged in it?

—No; I have heard of it from the warriors.

—When the great crowds of your young men crossed the river in front of the Long Hair, what did they do? Did they attempt to assault him directly in his front?

—At first they did, but afterward they found it better to try and get around him. They formed themselves on all sides of him, except just at his back.

—How long did it take them to put themselves around his flanks?

—As long as it takes the sun to travel from here to here (*indicating some marks upon his arm, with which, apparently, he is used to gauge the progress of the shadow of this lodge across his arm, and probably meaning half an hour. An Indian has no more definite way than this to express the lapse of time*).

—The trouble was with the soldiers, he continued; they were so exhausted, and their horses bothered them so much, that they could not take good aim. Some of their horses broke away from them and left them to stand and drop and die. When the Long Hair, the General, found that he was so outnumbered and threatened on his flanks, he took the best course he could have taken. The bugle blew. It was an order to fall back. All the men fell back fighting and dropping. They could not fire fast enough, though. But from our side it was so, *said Sitting Bull, and here he clapped his hands rapidly, twice a second, to express with what quickness and continuance the balls flew from the Henry and Winchester rifles wielded by the Indians.* They could not stand up under such a fire, *he added.*

—Were any military tactics shown? Did the Long Haired Chief make any disposition of his soldiers, or did it seem as though they retreated altogether, helter-skelter, fighting for their lives?

—They kept in pretty good order. Some great chief must have commanded them all the while. They would fall back across a coulee, and make a fresh stand beyond, on higher ground. The map is pretty nearly right. It shows where the white men stopped and fought before they were all killed. I think that is right—down there to the left, just above the Little Bighorn. There was one party driven out there, away from the rest, and there a great many men were killed. The places marked on the map are pretty nearly the places where all were killed.

—Did the whole command keep on fighting until the last?

—Every man, so far as my people could see. There were no cowards on either side.

—Cowards! One would think not.

I inquired of Sitting Bull: How long did this big fight continue?

—The sun was there, *he answered, pointing to within two hours of from the western horizon.*

I went on to interrogate Sitting Bull:

—This big fight, then, extended through three hours?

—Through most of the going forward of the sun.

—Where was the Long Hair most of the time?

—I have talked with my people; I cannot find one who saw the Long Hair until just before he died. He did not wear his hair long as he used to wear it. His hair was like yours, *Sitting Bull said, playfully touching my forehead with his finger.* It was short, but it was of the color of the grass when the frost comes.

—Did you hear from your people how he died? Did he die on horseback?

—No; none of them died on horseback.

—All were dismounted?

—Yes.

—And Custer, the Long Hair?

—Well, I have understood that there were a great many brave men in that fight, and that from time to time, while it was going on, they were shot down like pigs. They could not help themselves. One by one the officers fell. I believe the Long Hair rode across once from this place down here (*meaning the place where Tom Custer's and Smith's companies were killed*), to this place up here (*indicating the spot on the map where Custer fell*), but I am not sure about this. Any way it was said that up there, where the last fight took place, where the last stand was made, the Long Hair stood like a sheaf of corn with all the ears fallen around him.

—Not wounded?

—No.

—How many stood by him?

—A few.

—When did he fall?

—He killed a man when he fell. He laughed.

—You mean he cried out?

—No, he laughed; he had fired his last shot.

—From a carbine?

—No, a pistol.

—Did he stand up after he first fell?

—He rose up on his hands and tried another shot, but his pistol would not go off.

—Was any one else standing up when he fell down?

—One man was kneeling, that was all. But he died before the Long Hair. All this was far up on the bluffs, far away from the Sioux encampment. I did not see it. It was told to me. But it is true.

—The Long Hair was not scalped?

—No; my people did not want his scalp.

—Why?

—I have said he was a great chief.

—Did you at any time, *I persisted,* during the progress of the fight, believe that your people would get the worst of it?

—At one time, as I have told you, I started down to tell the squaws to strike the lodges. I was then on my way up to the right end of the camp, where the first attack was made upon us. But before I reached that end of the camp, where the Miniconjou and Hunkpapa squaws and children were, and where some of the other squaws—Cheyennes and Oglalas—had gone, I was overtaken by one of the young warriors, who had just come from the fight. He called out to me. He said: No use to leave camp; every white man is killed. So I stopped and went no further. I turned back, and by-and-by I met the warriors returning.

—But in the meantime, *I asked,* were there no warriors occupied up here at the right end of camp? Was nobody left except the squaws and the children and the old men to take care of that end of the camp? Was nobody ready to defend it against the soldiers in those intrenchments up there?

—Oh, *replied Sitting Bull again,* there was no need to waste warriors in that direction. There were only a few soldiers in those intrenchments, and we knew they wouldn't dare to come out.

This finished the interview, and with a few more How! Hows!, the wily chieftain withdrew.

Interviewed through an interpreter by a reporter of a leading newspaper.
Taken from "Wild Life on the Plains."

The opening shots of the battle, fired by three leading warriors (*only two are shown*) on Reno's cavalry. Amos Bad Heart Buffalo's painting catches the orderly drill-like charge that was soon to become a rout. Translated, the inscription reads:

> "These are the ones from up the river (*Reno's command*). This is the way the Indians met them (*the word used implies that the soldiers were shot from their horses*). The three who met them first were Kicking Bear (Mato Wanartaka), Hard to Hit (Oosicela), and Bad Heart Bull (Tatanka Cante Sica)."

> "I can't say that I, or anyone else was in command. I was sitting in my lodge, and all at once I heard the cry sounded, 'They are coming,' and everybody rushed for their guns and horses. When I went for my horse they were running away. As soon as I caught them my plan was to try and head off the soldiers from the creek, so I circled around on the outside for that purpose. Everybody was fighting, and pretty soon I heard women on the hill shouting, 'Daycia! Daycia!' 'Here they are!' Then I saw some soldiers in that direction, and the women running that way too, and we kept circling around and around them. I caught a lot of soldier horses and hurried with them to my lodge, but when I got back, every man was killed."

Statement of Chief Gall to Francis Holley,
Magazine Writer, published 1890

CHIEF GALL: his account

"How long before all the soldiers were killed?" *The chief made the sign of the white man's dinner time which means noon, and then with his finger cut in half, which would signify half an hour consumed in slaughtering everybody.*

"Did the men shoot guns or arrows?"

"Both. We soon shot all our cartridges, and then shot arrows and used our war clubs."

"Did the soldiers have plenty of ammunition?"

"No. They shot away all they had. The horses ran away, carrying in the saddle pockets a heap more. The soldiers threw their guns aside and fought with the little guns (*pistols*)."

"Who got the horses?"

"The Cheyenne women. A lot of horses got into the river and I jumped in and caught them."

The chief's mind seemed to dwell particularly upon the number of horses they captured rather than the terrible slaughter which took place.

"Did the Indians fight standing up?"

"No. The soldiers did, but the braves fired from behind their horses. A lot of Indians fell over and died."

"When the soldiers had no more cartridges left what did the Indians do?"

"The braves ran up to the soldiers and killed them with hatchets."

"How many Indians were killed?"

"Eleven down in that creek, four over there and two in that coulee."

"How many were killed, altogether?"

adapted from a drawing by Lisle Reedstrom

"Forty-three in all. A great many crossed the river and died in the rushes. They died every day. Nearly as many died every day as were killed in the fight. We buried them in trees and on scaffolds going up Lodge Pole Creek towards the White Rain Mountains."

"How many different tribes were in the fight?"

"Hunkpapa, Miniconjou, Oglala, Brule, Teton, Santee and Yanktonnais Sioux, Blackfeet, Cheyennes, Arapahoes, and a few Gros Ventres."

"Who fought first, Custer or Reno?"

"Reno was whipped first and then all with Custer were killed."

Of course the chief did not understand the names Custer and Reno, but he indicated by pointing and other signs who he meant.

"How soon after Reno charged did Custer come down the valley?"

"We saw all at one time before they separated. When Reno charged, the women and children were moved down stream: and when the Sioux bucks drove Reno to the top of the bluffs, everybody came down and fought Custer. All the Indians were mixed up then."

"How soon after Reno charged was Custer attacked?"

No satisfactory answer could be gotten to this important question; but it would seem that as soon as Reno was lodged safely on the hill the whole village massed on Custer at once and annihilated him.

"Did Custer get near the river?"

"No."

"Then how came the dead bodies of soldiers on the river's bank where we think the white chief crossed or attempted to cross?" *Gall's answer came without a moment's hesitation.*

"They were soldiers who fled down another coulee, crossed the river lower down, were chased up stream again toward the village, driven back into the river, and killed on this side."

"Did the soldiers fight on horseback or on foot?"

"They fought on foot. One man held the horses while the others shot the guns. We tried to kill the holders, and then by waving blankets and shouting we scared the horses down the coulee, where the Cheyenne women caught them."

"Did you kill any soldiers?"

"Yes. I killed a great many. I killed them all with the hatchet. I did not use a gun."

"Who had command of all the red men?"

"I held command of those down stream."

"Who was the first one killed with Reno?"

"I don't know; but some of the Sioux say it was a Crow (Arikara) scout named Bloody Knife."

"Where was Sitting Bull all this time while the white soldiers were being killed?"

"Back in his tepee making medicine."

"Did he fight at all?"

"No, he made medicine for us."

"Did you fight Reno?"

"No, I only fought the white men soldiers down this way."

"Then you know nothing of what happened at the upper end of the village?"

"No, I was down among the Cheyennes looking after horses when the first attack was made on our village."

"Did the old men and boys fight too?"

"Yes, and the squaws fought with stone clubs and hatchet knives.

The squaws cut off the boot legs."

"Were there any white men or breeds in your camp?"

"No; we had only Indians."

"Did the soldiers have swords?"

"No, there was only one long knife with them, and he was killed too."

"Who had the long knife?"

"I don't know."

"Did you see Curly on that day?" (*Pointing out the Crow scout who is the only survivor of all who marched with Custer into Little Big Horn valley.*)

"No, but my braves say he ran away early and did not fight at all."

"Did you take any prisoners, and if so what did you do with them?"

This question was put to find out if possible the true fate of Lieutenants Harrington, Jack Sturgis, Dr. Lord, and about fourteen others whose bodies were not found on the field, nor has anything been heard of them since the morning when the command was divided.

"No, we took no prisoners. Our hearts were bad, and we cut and shot them all to pieces."

"Do you remember seeing Custer, the big chief, after the fight?"

"I saw the big chief riding with the orderly before we attacked. He had glasses to his face (*field glasses*). During the fight there were too many soldiers scattered all around for me to see him."

"Did any of the soldiers get away?"

"No, all were killed. About fourteen (*indicating the number with his fingers*) started toward the Wolf Mountains, but the young braves got on their trail and all were killed."

No doubt Harrington, Sturgis, Lord and the other missing ones were of this party endeavoring to escape toward the Wolf Mountains.

"What did you do after all Custer's soldiers were killed?"

"We went back to fight the soldiers on the hill who were digging holes in the ground. We stayed there until big dust was seen down the river, when we all moved up Lodge Pole Creek toward the White Rain Mountains."

Hunkpapa Chief Gall attended the tenth anniversary observance at Custer Battlefield in June 1886. An interview with him was published in the St. Paul (Minn.) *Pioneer Press* of July 18, 1886.

These next two drawings follow the painting reproduced on the preceding page, continuing Amos's version of Reno's part in the battle. They show the same three warriors turning the troopers, who are retreating at a gallop.

Kicking Bear

"I went over with the others and peeped over the hills and saw the soldiers advancing . . . they seemed to fill the whole hill. It looked as if there were thousands of them, and I thought we would surely be beaten."

—Chief Runs-The-Enemy, Sioux

CHIEF RUNS-THE-ENEMY: his account

I fought at the Custer fight with a band of one hundred and thirty-two Cattle-Sioux under me. With the bravery and success I had had in former battles I was able to command the force at this fight.

We were encamped for two days in the valley of the Little Big Horn. The third day we were going to break camp and move farther along, but the old men went through the camp saying they were going to stay there still another day. After the cry had gone through the camp that we were to remain, the horses were all turned loose and were feeding on the hills north and west and south, and we were resting in the camp. Everything was quiet. I went over to the big tepee where there were several leading men, and we were sitting there talking and smoking. About ten o'clock a band of Sioux, who had been visiting the camp and had gone home, came rushing back with the tidings that the soldiers were coming. We could hardly believe that the soldiers were so near, and we were not very much depressed because of the report for two reasons: the soldiers had gone back to Wyoming, and we did not think they were near enough to attack us; and from the history of all our tribe, away back for generations, it had never been known that soldiers or Indians had attacked a Sioux camp in the daytime; they had always waited for night to come. And still we sat there smoking.

In a short time we heard the report of rifles, and bullets whizzed through the camp from the other side of the river. I left my pipe and ran as hard as I could, as did all the others, to our tents. As I ran to my tent there was a scream ran through the camp: ''The soldiers are here! The soldiers are here!'' The Indians who were herding the horses on the hill rushed to the camp with the horses, and the dust raised just like smoke. When I got to my tent the men who were herding the horses had got the horses there, and they were screaming. I grabbed my gun and cartridge belt, and the noise and confusion was so great that we did not know what we were doing. The women were running to the hills, and my heart was mad. The guns were still firing in the upper part of the camp. I did not have time to put on my war-bonnet; I jumped on the horse I had and made a pull for where the firing was.

The first thing I saw when I got to the battle line was a horse with a bridle on with the lines hanging down, and a dead Sioux. When I got to the line of battle—I thought I was quick, but I found a lot of Sioux already there—they were rushing on up the hill. We were all naked, and the soldiers with their pack saddles and their uniforms on and their black horses looked like great big buffalo.

The Sioux were all riding up on the hill. We saw one lone Indian on the hill going down toward the soldiers and the river. We could not see him as he came down the hill, but we could see the smoke coming from under his horse's head, and we all thought that he was going to make a charge on the soldiers, and we all charged. It seemed as though that one Indian had the attention of all the soldiers, and they were all firing at him. When we saw that the smoke was all going toward the soldiers, that gave us a chance to charge from this side, and we all made a rush.

When we made the charge we got them all stampeded. For smoke and dust we could not see the soldiers as they retreated toward the river. The Sioux were fresh, and we soon caught up with them. We passed a black man in a soldier's uniform and we had him. He turned on his horse and shot an Indian right through the heart. Then the Indians fired at this one man, and riddled his horse with bullets. His horse fell over on his back, and the black man could not get up. I saw him as I rode by. I afterward saw him lying there dead. We fought them until they rolled and tumbled and finally had to go into the river, which was very deep. We made them cross the river. The country around the river in those days was very heavily wooded. We chased some of the soldiers into the woods, and others across the river and up the hill.

I did not know the name of the commander of the soldiers at that time, but I afterward heard that it was Reno. I also heard afterward that they had a big trial and charged him with being a coward, but I praised him for rushing into the camp. The reason I praised him was that he only had a few soldiers and our camp was a great camp, and he came rushing into the camp with his few soldiers. In all the history of my great-grandfather I have never known of such an attack in daylight. After they retreated over the hills and we had killed a large number of them, that battle was ended. I was at the Custer Battlefield this morning, and I noticed there were no monuments up for the soldiers who fell on the Reno Field.

As we finished with the Reno battle and were returning to camp we saw two men on the Reno Hills waving two blankets as hard as they could. Two of us rode over to where they were, and they yelled to us that the genuine stuff was coming, and they were going to get our women and children. I went over with the others and peeped over the hills and saw the soldiers advancing. As I looked along the line of the ridge they seemed to fill the whole hill. It looked as if there were thousands of them, and I thought we would surely be beaten. As I returned I saw hundreds of Sioux. I looked into their eyes and they looked different—they were filled with fear. I then called my one band together, and I took off the ribbons from my hair, also my shirt and pants, and threw them away, saving nothing but my belt of cartridges and gun. I thought, most of the Sioux will fall today; I will fall with them. Just at that time Sitting Bull made his appearance. He said, just as though I could hear him at this moment: "A bird, when it is on its nest, spreads its wings to cover the nest and eggs and protect them. It cannot use its wings for defense, but it can cackle and try to drive away the enemy. We are here to protect our wives and children, and we must not let the soldiers get them." He was on a buckskin horse, and he rode from one end of the line to the other, calling out: "Make a brave fight!"

We were all hidden along the ridge of hills. While Sitting Bull was telling this I looked up and saw that the Cheyennes had made a circle around Custer on the west, north, and east sides, and that left a gap on the south side for us to fill. We then filled up the gap, and as we did so we looked over to the Cheyenne side, and there was a woman among the Cheyennes who was nearest the soldiers trying to fight them. While Custer was all surrounded, there had been no firing from either side. The Sioux then made a charge from the rear side, shooting into the men, and the shooting frightened the horses so that they rushed upon the ridge and many horses were shot. The return fire was so strong that the Sioux had to retreat back over the hill again. I left my men there and told them to hold that position, and then I rushed around the hills and came up to the north end of the field near where the monument now stands. And I saw hundreds and hundreds of Indians in the coulees all around. The Indians dismounted and tied their horses in a bunch and got down into the coulees, shooting at the soldiers from all sides. From the point that juts out just below where the monument stands about thirty of us got through the line, firing as we went, and captured a lot of Custer's horses and drove them down to the river. The horses were so thirsty that the moment we reached the river they just stood and drank and drank, and that gave us a chance to get off our horses and catch hold of the bridles. They were all loaded with shells and blankets and everything that the soldiers carried with them.

Then I returned to my men, and the soldiers were still on the hill fighting, with some of their horses near them. Just as I got back, some of the soldiers made a rush down the ravine toward the river, and a great roll of smoke seemed to go down the ravine. This retreat of the soldiers down the ravine was met by the advance of the Indians from the river, and all who were not killed came back again to the hill.

After the soldiers got back from the hills they made a stand all in a bunch. Another charge was made and they retreated along the line of the ridge; it looked like a stampede of buffalo. On this retreat along the ridge, the soldiers now broke the line and divided, some of them going down the eastern slope of the hill, and some of them going down to the river. The others came back to where the final stand was made on the hill, but they were few in number then. The soldiers then gathered in a group, where the monument now stands—I visited the monument today and confirmed my memory of it—and then the soldiers and Indians were all mixed up. You could not tell one from the other. In this final charge I took part and when the last soldier was killed the smoke rolled up like a mountain above our heads, and the soldiers were piled one on top of another, dead, and here and there an Indian among the soldiers. I saw one that had been hit across the head with a war axe, and others had been hit with arrows. After we were done, we went back to the camp.

After the onslaught I did not see any soldiers scalped, but I saw the Indians piling up their clothes, and there was shooting all over the hill, for the Indians were looking for the wounded soldiers and were shooting them dead. Just as I got back to the camp I heard that a packtrain was coming from over the hills. I looked over the hills and saw the Sioux and Cheyennes moving that way. I remained a little while to look after my wife and children. After I had located my family, I fired off my shells and got a new supply of ammunition and went toward the packtrain.

When I got over there the fighting had begun. The packtrain had fortified itself by making entrenchments. The Indians were on the outside firing into it, and the soldiers were firing at the Indians. During this last fight the sun was getting low. After it grew dark the firing continued; you would see the flash of the guns in the entrenchments. The Indians would crawl up and fire a flock of arrows into the entrenchments and then scatter away. This kept up all night. I did not stay, but went home.

The next morning I went over there and found that the Indians had the packtrain surrounded and the fight was still going on. We kept at long range and continued our firing. The soldiers were all sharpshooters, and the moment we put our heads up they fired at us and nearly hit us. The news went around among all the Indians that they were to stay there, and that all the soldiers in the entrenchment would be so dry soon that they would have to get out and we would get them. I cannot quite remember, but I think it was about noon—we held them until then—when news came from our camp down on the plain that there was a big bunch of soldiers coming up the river: General Terry with his men. As soon as we heard this we let the packtrain go and fled back to our camp. We at once broke camp and fled up the Little Bighorn, or Greasy Creek, as it is called by the Indians. If it had not been for General Terry coming up as he did we would have had that packtrain, for they were all dry—they had had no water for two days.

After we had killed Custer and all his men I did not think very much about it. The soldiers fired first and we returned the fire. Sitting Bull had talked to us and all the tribes to make a brave fight and we made it. When we had killed all the soldiers we felt that we had done our duty, and felt that it was a great battle and not a massacre. With reference to the real reason for this fight I may say that the talk among the Indians was that they were going to compel us to stay on the reservation and take our country away from us . Our purpose was to move north and go as far north as possible away from the tribes. Our object was not to fight the Crows or any other tribe, but we learned that the soldiers were getting after us to try to compel us to go back on the reservation, and we were trying to get away from them. During the Custer fight our tents were not attacked, but after the battle the women gathered up their dead husbands and brothers, and laid them out nicely in the tepee, and left them. I understand that after we had left the tepees standing, holding our dead, the soldiers came and burned the tepees.

According to my estimate there were about two thousand

able-bodied warriors engaged in this fight; they were all in good fighting order. The guns and ammunition that we gathered from the dead soldiers of Custer's command put us in better fighting condition than ever before, but the sentiment ran around among the Indians that we had killed enough, and we did not want to fight anymore. There has been a good deal of dispute about the number of Indians killed. About the closest estimate that we can make is that fifty Sioux were killed in the fight, and others died a short time afterward from their wounds.

Taken down in Sept. 1909 by Dr. Joseph K. Dixon and published in *The Vanishing Race.*

"... they (*the soldiers*) did very poor shooting. They held their horses' reins on one arm while they were shooting but their horses were so frightened that they pulled the men all around, and a great many of their shots went up in the air and did us no harm."

—*Low Dog*

Reno's move from the first defense position is depicted in this painting by Amos Bad Heart Buffalo.

LOW DOG: his account

We were in camp near Little Big Horn River. We had lost some horses, and an Indian went back on the trail to look for them. We did not know that the white warriors were coming after us. Some scouts or men in advance of the warriors saw the Indian looking for the horses and ran after him and tried to kill him to keep him from bringing us word, but he ran faster than they and came into camp and told us that the white warriors were coming.

I was asleep in my lodge at the time. The sun was about noon (*pointing with his finger*). I heard the alarm. I did not think it possible that any white men would attack us, so strong as we were. We had in camp the Cheyennes, Arapahoes, and seven different tribes of the Teton Sioux—a countless number. Although I did not believe it was a true alarm, I lost no time getting ready. When I got my gun and came out of my lodge the attack had begun at the end of the camp where Sitting Bull and the Hunkpapas were. The Indians held their ground to give the women and children time to get out of the way. By this time the herders were driving in the horses and as I was nearly at the further end of the camp, I ordered my men to catch their horses and get out of the way, and my men were hurrying to go and help those that were fighting.

When the fighters saw that the women and children were safe they fell back. By this time my people went to help them, and the less able warriors and the women caught horses and got them ready, and we drove the first attacking party back, and that party retreated to a high hill. Then I told my people not to venture too far in pursuit for fear of falling into an ambush. By this time all the warriors in our camp were mounted and ready for fight, and then we were attacked on the other side by another party. They came on us like a thunderbolt. I never

before or since saw men so brave and fearless as those white warriors. We retreated until our men got all together, and then we charged upon them. I called to my men, "This is a good day to die: follow me." We massed our men, and that no man should fall back, every man whipped another man's horse and we rushed right upon them.

As we rushed upon them the white warriors dismounted to fire, but they did very poor shooting. They held their horses' reins on one arm while they were shooting but their horses were so frightened that they pulled the men all around, and a great many of their shots went up in the air and did us no harm. The white warriors stood their ground bravely, and none of them made any attempt to get away. After all but two of them were killed, I captured two of their horses. Then the wise men and chiefs of our nation gave out to our people not to mutilate the dead white chief, for he was a brave warrior and died a brave man, and his remains should be respected.

Then I turned around and went to help fight the other white warriors, who had retreated to a high hill on the east side of the river . . . I don't know whether any white men of Custer's force were taken prisoners. When I got back to our camp they were all dead. Everything was in confusion all the time of the fight. I did not see General Custer. I do not know who killed him. We did not know till the fight was over that he was the white chief. We had no idea that the white warriors were coming until the runner came in and told us. I do not say that Reno was a coward. He fought well, but our men were fighting to save their women and children, and drive them back. If Reno and his warriors had fought as Custer and his warriors fought, the battle might have been against us. No white man or Indian ever fought as bravely as

Custer and his men. The next day we fought Reno and his forces again and killed many of them. Then the chiefs said these men had been punished enough, and that we ought to be merciful, and let them go. Then we heard that another force was coming up the river to fight us . . . and we started to fight them, but the chiefs and wise men counseled that we had fought enough and that we should not fight unless attacked, and we went back and took our women and children and went away.

. . . When Low Dog began his narrative, only Captain Howe, the interpreter, and myself were present, but as he progressed the officers gathered round, listening to every word, and all were impressed that the Indian chief was giving a true account, according to his knowledge. Some one asked how many Indians were killed in the fight; Low Dog answered, "Thirty-eight, who died then, and a great many—I can't tell the number—who were wounded and died afterwards. I never saw a fight in which so many in proportion to the killed were wounded, and so many horses were wounded."

Another asked who were the dead Indians that were found in two tepees—five in one and six in another—all richly dressed, and with their ponies, slain about the tepees. He said eight were chiefs killed in battle. One was his own brother, born of the same mother and the same father, and he did not know who the other two were.

The question was asked, "What part did Sitting Bull take in the fight?" Low Dog is not friendly to Sitting Bull. He answered with a sneer: "If someone would lend him a heart he would fight." Then Low Dog said he would like to go home, and with the interpreter he went back to the Indian camp. He is a tall, straight Indian, thirty-four years old, not a bad face, regular features and small hands and feet. He said that when he had his weapons and was on the warpath he considered no man his superior; but when he surrendered he laid that feeling aside, and now if any man should try to chastise him in his humble condition and helplessness all he could do would be to tell him that he was no man and a coward; which, while he was on the warpath he would allow no man to say and live.

In July 1881 reporters interviewed the Oglala Sioux Chief Low Dog at Standing Rock Agency, Dakota Territory. The account was published in the *Leavenworth* (Kansas) *Weekly Times* of August 18, 1881.

Reno's command has dismounted after the first exchange of shots, and is fighting from the woods.

"There was such a rush and mix-up that it seemed the whole world had gone wild. There was so much dust and smoke in the air, that I did not see what happened . . ."

—*Kate Bighead*

"The warriors around them (*the soldiers*) were shifting from shelter to shelter, each one of them trying to get close enough to strike a coup blow of some kind upon a living enemy, as all warriors try to do when in a fight."

—*Kate Bighead*

CHIEF RED CLOUD: his account

I remember that our camp was located in the valley of the Little Big Horn. As I remember there were about four thousand Indians in our camp, and about a hundred Sioux warriors in my own band. There were four or five different sections of the Sioux tribe in this fight. I remember that Rain-in-the-Face and Sitting Bull, Crazy Horse, and Big Man were with us in the battle. We were in our camp; there was plenty of buffalo meat in those days, and we killed a good many. The women were drying the meat, and the warriors were resting. Suddenly we heard firing, and we found out that the soldiers were on us. The women and children were all frightened, and started to run across the hills, and we men mounted our horses and started toward the enemy.

I remember that we pushed Reno back until he had to cross the river, and go up against the bluffs, and then some of our Sioux rode around the hill to head him off, and we had him in a pocket. After we had killed many of Reno's men, Custer came along the ridge, and we were called off to fight Custer. We kept circling around Custer, and as his men came down the ridge we shot them down. And then the rest dismounted and gathered in a bunch, kneeling down and shooting from behind the horses. We circled round and round, firing into Custer's men until the last man was killed. I did not see Custer fall, for all the Indians did not know which was Custer. One reason why we did not scalp Custer was because the Indians and the white soldiers were so mixed up that it was hard to distinguish one man from another; and another reason was because Custer was the bravest man of all and we did not want to touch him as he made the last stand. This is also the opinion of Rain-in-the-Face.

Regarding the cause of the Custer fight I must say, we

were pursued by the soldiers, we were on the warpath, and we were on the warpath with the Crows and other tribes. We were trying to drive them back from the hunting grounds, and the soldiers came upon us and we had to defend ourselves. We were driven out of the Black Hills by the men seeking gold, and our game was driven off, and we started on our journey in search of game. Our children were starving, and we had to have something to eat. There was buffalo in that region and we were moving, simply camping here and there and fighting our Indian enemies as we advanced, in order to get the game that was in this country. We fought this battle from daylight up until three o'clock in the afternoon, and all of the white men were killed. I think that Custer was a very brave man to fight all these Indians with his few men from daylight until the sun was almost going down.

Taken down in Sept. 1909 by Dr. Joseph K. Dixon, and published in *The Vanishing Race.*

DEWEY BEARD (Wasu Masa): his account

Hump, Fast Bull, and High Backbone led my tribe. Crazy Horse headed the Oglala. Inkpaduta (Scarlet Tip) led the Santee. Lame White Man and Ice Bear led the Cheyenne. But the greatest leader of all was the chief of the Hunkpapa—Sitting Bull. As long as we were all camped together, we looked on him as head chief. We all rallied around him because he stood for our old way of life and the freedom we had always known. We were not there to make war, but, if need be, we were ready to fight for our sacred rights. Since the white man's government had promised our leaders that we could wander and hunt in our old territory as long as the grass should grow, we did not believe the white soldiers had any business in our hunting grounds. Yet they came to attack us anyway.

I slept late that morning of the fight. The day before I had been hunting buffalo and I had to ride far to find the herds because there were so many people in the valley. I came back with meat, but I was very tired. So when I got up, the camp women were already starting out to dig for wild turnips. Two of my uncles had left early for another buffalo hunt. Only my grandmother and a third uncle were in the tepee, and the sun was high overhead and hot. I walked to the

after a painting by David Humphreys Miller

river to take a cool swim, then got hungry and returned to the tepee at dinner time (*noon*).

"When you finish eating," my uncle said, "go to our horses. Something might happen today. I feel it in the air."

I hurried to Muskrat Creek and joined my younger brother, who was herding the family horses. By the time I reached the herd, I heard shouting in the village. People were yelling that white soldiers were riding toward the camp.

I had no time to paint Zi Chischila properly for making war, just a minute or so to braid his tail and to daub a few white hail spots of paint on my own forehead for protection before I galloped out on the little buckskin to help defend the camp. I met four other Lakotas riding fast. Three were veteran fighters, armed with rifles; the other was young like me and carried a bow and arrows as I did. One of the veterans went down. I saw my chance to act bravely and filled the gap. We all turned when we heard shooting at the far side of the village nearest the Miniconjou camp circle and rode fast to meet this new danger. I could see swirls of dust and hear shooting on the hills and bluffs across the river. Hundreds of other warriors joined us as we splashed across the ford near our camp and raced up the hills to charge into the thickest of the fighting.

This new battle was a turmoil of dust and warriors and soldiers, with bullets whining and arrows hissing all around. Sometimes a bugle would sound and the shouting would get louder. Some of the soldiers were firing pistols at close range. Our knives and war clubs flashed in the sun. I could hear bullets whiz past my ears. But I kept going and

shouting, "It's a good day to die!" so that everyone who heard would know I was not afraid of being killed in battle.

Then a Lakota named Spotted Rabbit rode unarmed among us, calling out a challenge to all the warriors to join him. He shouted, "Let's take their leader alive!" I had no thought of what we would do with this leader once we caught him; it was a daring feat that required more courage and much more skill than killing him. I dug my heels into my pony's flanks to urge him on faster to take part in the capture.

The soldier chief we had tried to capture lay on the ground with the reins of his horse's bridle tied to his wrist. It was a fine animal, a blaze-faced sorrel with four white stockings. A Santee named Walks-Under-the-Ground took that horse. Then he told everyone that the leader lying there dead was Long Hair; so that was the first I knew who we had been fighting. I thought it was a strange name for a soldier chief who had his hair cut short.

Our attempt to save Long Hair's life had failed. But we all felt good about our victory over the soldiers and celebrated with a big scalp dance. But our triumph was hollow. A winter or so later more soldiers came to round us up on reservations. There were too many of them to fight now. We were split up into bands and no longer felt strong. At last we were ready for peace and believed we would have no more trouble.

From an interview conducted by David Humphreys Miller in 1935 and translated in his "Echoes of the Little Big Horn."

"The whole valley was filled with smoke, and the bullets flew all around us, making a noise like bees. . . . We could hardly hear anything for the noise of the guns. When the guns were firing, the Sioux and Cheyennes and soldiers, one falling one way and one falling another, together with the noise of the guns, I shall never forget . . ."
—*Chief Two Moons, Cheyenne leader*

CRAZY HORSE: his account

We did not ask you white men to come here. The Great Spirit gave us this country as a home. You had yours. We did not interfere with you. The Great Spirit gave us plenty of land to live on and buffalo, deer, antelope and other game; you are taking my land from me; you are killing off our game, so it is hard for us to live. Now you tell us to work for a living, but the Great Spirit did not make us to work, but to live by hunting. You white men can work if you want to. We do not interfere with you, and again you say, why do you not become civilized? We do not want your civilization! We would live as our fathers did, and their fathers before them.

I am no white man! They are the only people who make rules for other people, that say, "If you stay on one side of this line it is peace, but if you go on the other side, I will kill you all." I don't hold with deadlines. There is plenty of room; camp where you please."

The Plains Indians were more laconic than most, and Crazy Horse hardly ever spoke. He was known as a loner who went off by himself on one-man attacks against the Crows, and his hunting was almost always done alone. These few quotations, taken down by Major V.T. McGillicuddy, are all I can find that seem to be his words.

"... Crazy Horse was a chief of the Oglala and a brave fighter. He wore plain white buckskins and let his hair hang loose with no feathers in it. He had white spots painted here and there on his face for protection in battle, and it was said he was bulletproof."

—Joseph White Bull

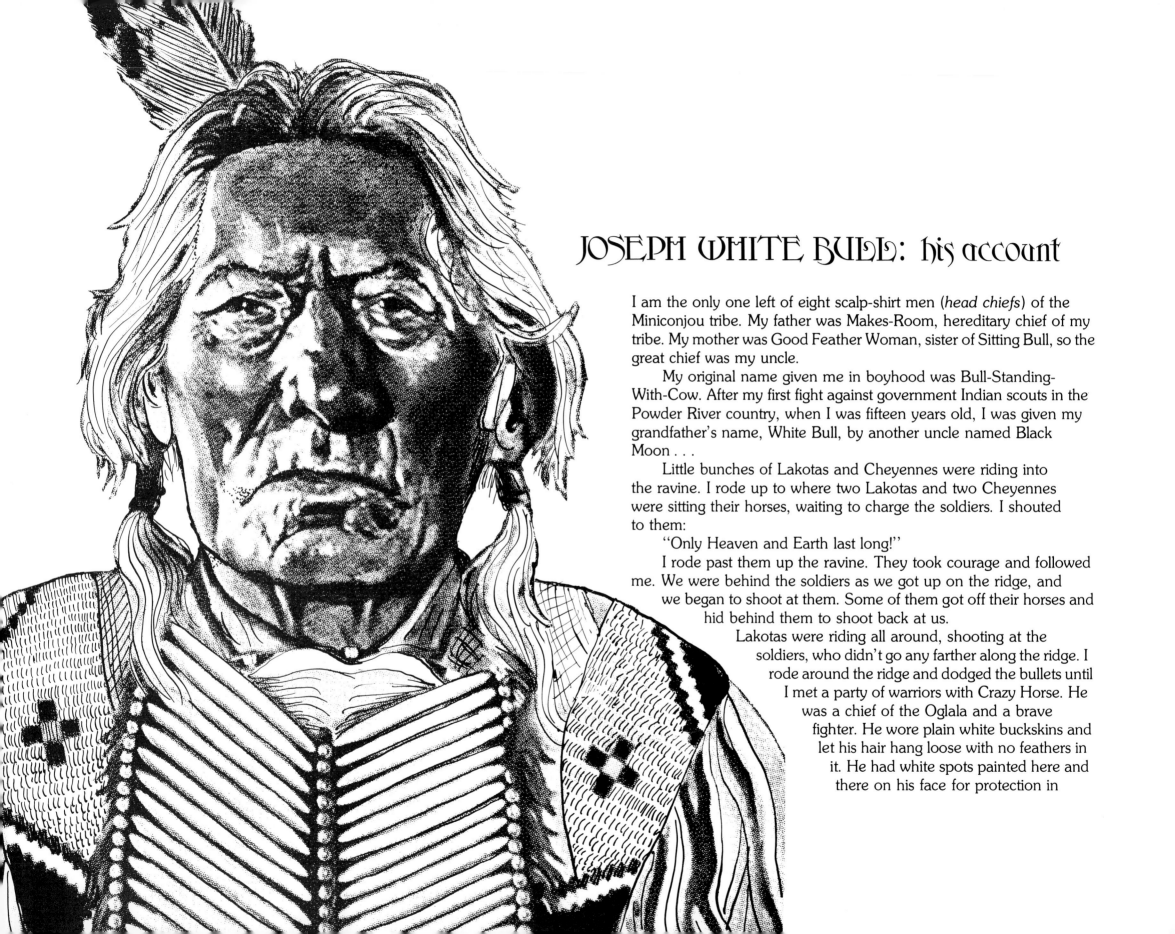

JOSEPH WHITE BULL: his account

I am the only one left of eight scalp-shirt men (*head chiefs*) of the Miniconjou tribe. My father was Makes-Room, hereditary chief of my tribe. My mother was Good Feather Woman, sister of Sitting Bull, so the great chief was my uncle.

My original name given me in boyhood was Bull-Standing-With-Cow. After my first fight against government Indian scouts in the Powder River country, when I was fifteen years old, I was given my grandfather's name, White Bull, by another uncle named Black Moon . . .

Little bunches of Lakotas and Cheyennes were riding into the ravine. I rode up to where two Lakotas and two Cheyennes were sitting their horses, waiting to charge the soldiers. I shouted to them:

"Only Heaven and Earth last long!"

I rode past them up the ravine. They took courage and followed me. We were behind the soldiers as we got up on the ridge, and we began to shoot at them. Some of them got off their horses and hid behind them to shoot back at us.

Lakotas were riding all around, shooting at the soldiers, who didn't go any farther along the ridge. I rode around the ridge and dodged the bullets until I met a party of warriors with Crazy Horse. He was a chief of the Oglala and a brave fighter. He wore plain white buckskins and let his hair hang loose with no feathers in it. He had white spots painted here and there on his face for protection in battle, and it was said he was bulletproof.

The soldiers were divided into two bunches. I galloped my pony in between the two bunches and kept close to his neck until I rode clear around one of the bunches and circled back to Crazy Horse. I shouted to him:

"Hoka hey, brother! This life will not last forever!"

I started to circle the soldiers again. This time Crazy Horse and the others followed. Some of the soldiers ran like scared rabbits, and we rode after them. One soldier was riding a black horse. A Lakota on foot shot him, and he fell off the horse. I ran up to strike him with my quirt.

One of the soldiers blew on a bugle. The others began to get on their horses. I dared Crazy Horse to lead a charge against them. He refused, so I rode out alone and came up behind a soldier on a bay horse. I grabbed his coat and pulled him out of his saddle. He tried to shoot me, but his rifle fired into the air; he fell screaming to the ground. I rode down two soldiers and lashed them with my quirt. Crazy Horse struck both of these men after I did.

One soldier fired his rifle at me, then threw it at my head. He tried to wrestle with me. I had a bad time keeping him from getting my rifle. He began hitting me on the face. Then he grabbed my long hair in his hands and tried to bite my nose off!

One soldier still alive toward the last wore a buckskin coat with fringes on it. I thought this man was leader of the soldiers, because he had ridden ahead of all the others as they came along the ridge. He saw me now and shot at me twice with his revolver, missing me both times. I raised my rifle and fired at him; he went down. Then I saw another soldier crawl over to him. The leader was dead.

By the middle of the afternoon all the soldiers were dead. The fight lasted only a short time. All of us were crazy. We had killed many soldiers. They had attacked us and meant to wipe us out. We were fighting for our lives and homeland. Cries of victory went up. Our women came through the timber by the river and began to strip the dead soldiers.

Some of the Lakotas said they found whiskey bottles on the soldiers after the fight. The soldiers had acted like drunk people.

My cousin Bad Soup was stripping the soldier I thought had been the leader and held up the buckskin coat. He looked in the pockets of the coat and brought out some papers with pictures on them (maps). In one of the pockets he found coils of long yellow hair. But the dead leader had his hair cut short.

"Onhey!" Bad Soup cried. "That man was Long Hair Custer. He thought he was the greatest man on earth, but he lies there now. And he cut his hair so he would not be scalped!"

He was the leader who had tried to kill me. But I had killed him . . .

From an interview conducted by David Humphreys Miller in 1939 and translated in his "Echoes of the Little Big Horn."

The retreating soldiers are shown nearing the river. There is apparently time, at this stage of the fight, for the Indians to stop and strip the fallen soldiers (center, lower right). Note the tied-up tail of the Indian ponies. This was typical Sioux practice before battle.

"... I came to a group of four dead soldiers; one of them had on a red flannel shirt, the other three had red stripes on the arm, one had three stripes, the other had three stripes and a sword. When I turned back I could not see anything but soldiers and Indians all mixed up together. You could hardly tell one from the other ..." —*Chief Two Moons*

SHEET PAINTED TO REPRESENT CUSTER'S BATTLE, made about 1890 by an anon. Sioux—
Courtesy of Museum of the American Indian, Heye Foundation

CHIEF TWO MOONS
(Cheyenne Leader): his account

Custer came up along the ridge and across the mountains from the right of the monument. The Cheyenne and the Sioux came up the coulee from the foot of Reno Hill, and circled about. I led the Cheyennes as we came up. Custer marched up from behind the ridge on which his monument stands down into the valley until we could not see them. The Cheyennes and the Sioux came up to the right over in the valley of the Little Big Horn. Custer placed his men in groups along this ridge. They dismounted. The men who had dismounted along the ridge seemed to have let their horses go down the other side of the ridge. Those who were on the hill where the monument now stands, and where I am now standing, had gray horses where Long Hair stood.

I led the Cheyennes up the long line of ridge from the valley blocking the soldiers and I called to my Cheyenne brothers: "Come on children; do not be scared!" And they came after me, yelling and firing. We broke the line of soldiers and went over the ridge. Another band of Indians and Sioux came from over beyond the ridge, and when I got over there, I got off my white horse and told my men to wait, and we loaded our guns and fired into the first troop which was very near us. At the first volley the troop at which we fired were all killed. We kept firing along the ridge on which the troops were stationed and kept advancing.

I rode my horse back along the ridge again and called upon my children to come on after me. Many of my Cheyenne brothers were killed, and I whipped my horse and told them to come on, that this was the last day they would ever see their chief, and I again started for the bunch of gray horses on the hilltop. The Indians followed me, yelling and firing. I could not break the line at the bunch of gray horses and I wheeled and went to the left down the

103

valley with the line of soldiers facing me as I went, firing at me, and all my men firing at the soldiers.

Then I rode on up the ridge to the left. I met an Indian with a big war-bonnet on, and right there I saw a soldier wounded. I killed him and jumped off my horse and scalped him. The Indian I met was Black Bear, a Cheyenne. I rode down the ridge and came to a group of four dead soldiers; one of them had on a red flannel shirt, the other three had red stripes on the arm, one had three stripes, the other had three stripes and a sword. They all had on good clothes, and I jumped off my horse and took their clothes and their guns. When I turned back I could not see anything but soldiers and Indians all mixed up together. You could hardly tell one from the other. As I rode along the ridge I found nearly all the soldiers killed. I again rode up to the ridge along which Custer's troops had been stationed. I found two or three killed and saw one running away to get on top of the high hills beyond, and we took after him, and killed him.

The whole valley was filled with smoke and the bullets flew all about us, making a noise like bees. We could hardly hear anything for the noise of the guns. When the guns were firing, the Sioux and Cheyennes and soldiers, one falling one way and one falling another, together with the noise of the guns, I shall never forget. At last we saw that Custer and his men were grouped on the side of the hill, and we commenced to circle round and round, the Sioux and Cheyennes, and we all poured in on Custer and his men, firing into them until the last man was shot. We then jumped off our horses, took their guns, and scalped them.

After the fight was over we gathered in the river bottom and cut willow sticks, then some Indians were delegated to go and throw down a stick wherever they found a dead soldier, and then they were ordered to pick up the sticks again, and in this way we counted the number of the dead. It was about six times we had to cut willow sticks, because we kept finding men all along the ridge. We counted four hundred and eighty-eight with our sticks along the ridge. We were trying to count the dead there in the valley when General Terry came up from the other side, and we fled away. After the battle was over, the Indians made a circle all over the ridges and around through the valley to see if they could find any more soldiers, as they were determined to kill every one. The next morning after the fight we went up behind the Reno Field and camped at Black Lodge River. We then followed the Black Lodge River until we came back to the Little Big Horn again. Then we camped at the Little Big Horn, moving our camp constantly, fearing pursuit by the soldiers.

Before the Custer fight we went over on the Tongue River and found a camp of soldiers. We rushed upon them and took all their horses away, and the soldiers ran into the brush. We knew there would be other soldiers after us; we knew about where they were, and we felt they would pursue us. At Powder River the soldiers attacked our camp and destroyed everything, and that made us mad. When the soldiers came after us, on the day of the Custer fight, we were ready to kill them all.

The soldiers were after us all the time, and we had to fight.

Taken down in Sept. 1909 by Dr. Joseph K. Dixon, and published in *The Vanishing Race.*

In the wild rush for the river, dead and wounded are left on the field as Amos Bad Heart Buffalo continues his pictorial history of Reno's retreat in the paintings reproduced on the following pages.

"I rode up behind one soldier and knocked him over with my war club. Then I slid off my pony and held the soldier's head under water until he was dead . . . ."
—*Henry Oscar One Bull*

"The Indians were using bows and arrows more than they were using guns. Many of them had no guns, and not many who did have them had also plenty of bullets. But even if they had been well supplied with both guns and bullets, in that fight the bow was better."

Kate Bighead

RENO'S RETREAT—drawing by White Bird—courtesy of West Point Museum

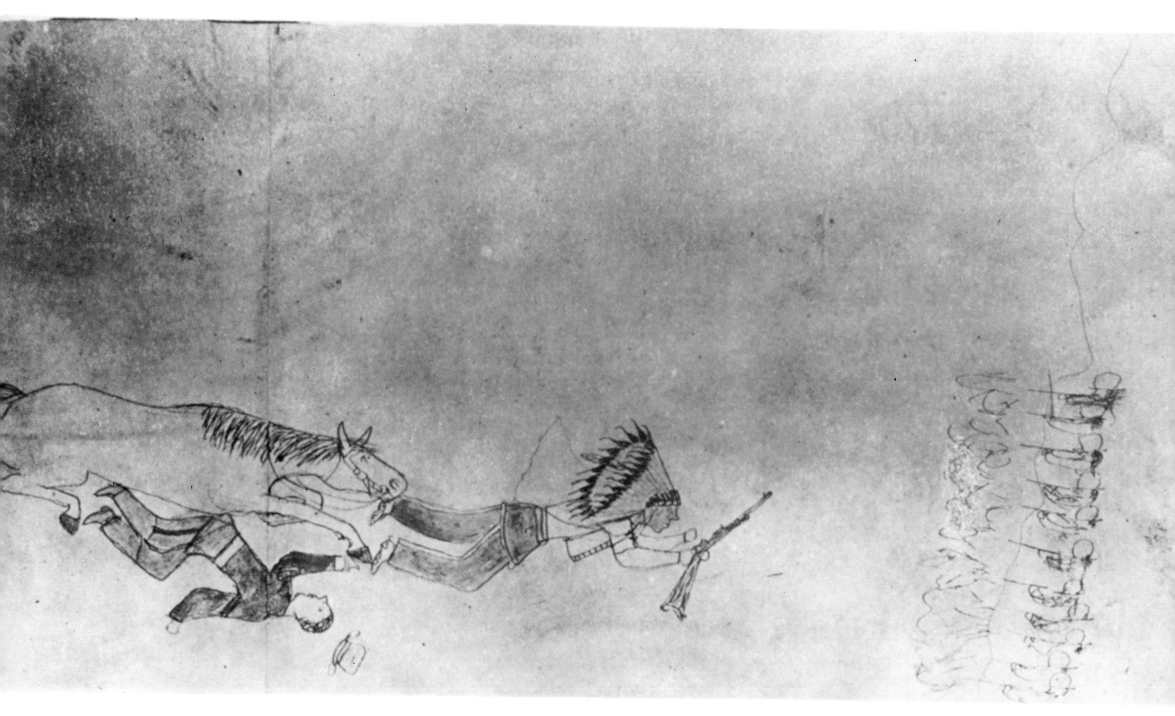

A scene of the tactics used to get close to the Reno-Benteen defense line as drawn by Amos Bad Heart Buffalo is reproduced above. A bonneted Sioux, having just killed the trooper on the left, crawls toward the barricaded soldiers on the right. White Bird's style of drawing the retreat could not be more different from Amos's, as is evident in the work reproduced on the facing page. There is a sense of calm on both sides suggestive of a scene from a play. 113

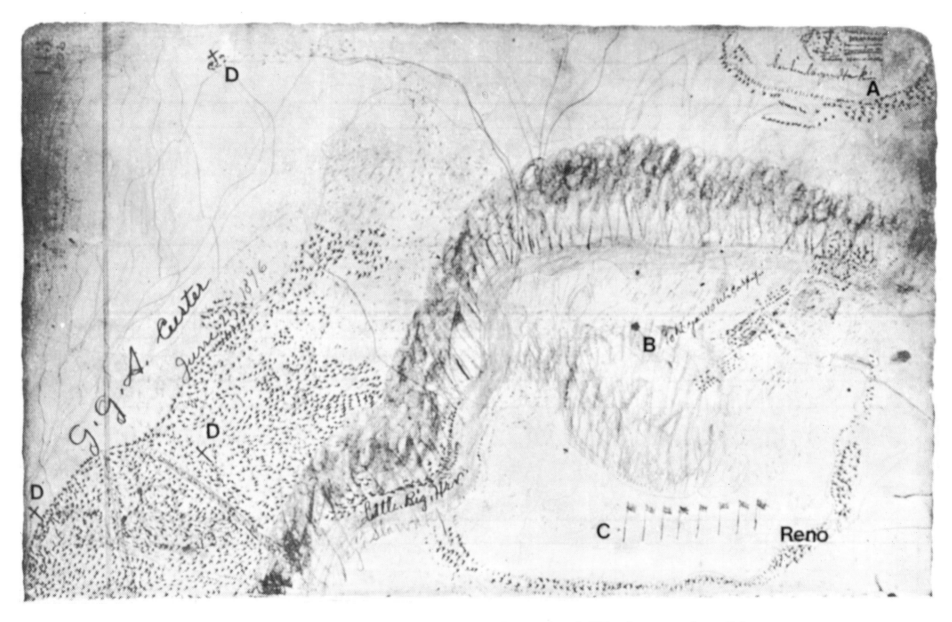

Amos Bad Heart Buffalo's detailed topographical map of the battle shows B translated: "The first ones shot off their horses." This refers to the first troopers shot when Reno was charging the encampment. A: The note here translated: "The ones who have the mules" (referring to the mule packtrain that found Reno and Benteen). C: Is the besieged Reno-Benteen group D: The two crosses in the thick of the Custer stand undoubtedly mark major events, supposedly the site of Custer's death. The cross at the top left of the map is thought to be the place of the last man's death.

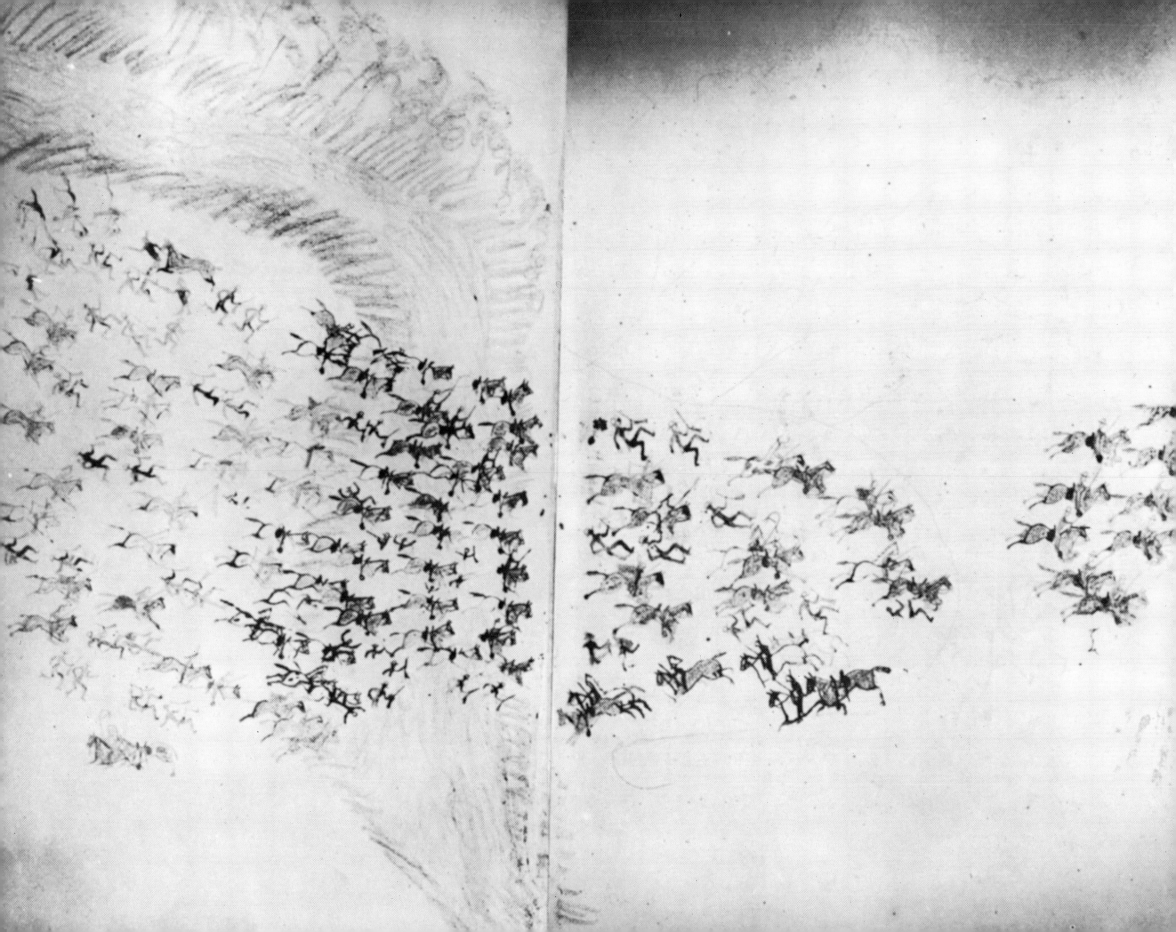

THE BATTLE OF THE LITTLE BIG HORN—by White Bird—Courtesy of West Point Museum

White Bird is presenting the same view—Custer surrounded on the left, with Benteen and Reno across the river on the right. Below are the Indian encampments. The small group of fallen soldiers at the right side of the wigwams at the bottom clearly indicates Reno's second defense line, with foot tracks to show his retreat across the river and up to the bluffs above.

The fate of some of Custer's Indian scouts is shown in this series of four drawings by Amos Bad Heart Buffalo. The translation of the inscription for the first picture, reproduced on the facing page, reads:

1. *Running Eagle shot him (from the rear) (lower left)*
2. *Young Skunk killed him (meaning that Young Skunk, the warrior in the fringed mantle, first struck the enemy's body, thus counting coup upon him) (upper center)*
3. *Runs Fearless (the warrior on the black horse) struck second (lower right)*

In the second picture, a mounted Ree scout is shown attacked by several Dakotas and Cheyennes. In the third, four Dakotas are leading captured cavalry horses from the battlefield.

Finally, in the last picture, Bad Heart Bull the Elder (Amos's father) is shown, wearing his personal charm of a fox skin. The translation of the inscription reads:

Bad Heart Bull killing. Bad Heart Bull the Elder counting coup upon one of the Ree scouts and killing him.

"I endured all the hardships the soldiers endured in order to hold my land. . . . Land is a very valuable thing, and especially our land. . . . We had hardships climbing mountains, fording rivers, frost and cold of winter, the burning heat of summer—my bones ache today from the exposure, but it was all for love of my home. I stood faithfully by the soldiers. They did not know the country. I did. They wanted me for their eye, they could not see. The soldiers were the same as though they were blind, and I used both of my own eyes for them. The soldiers and I were fighting in friendship; what they said, I did. So I helped my tribe."
—*White-Man-Runs-Him, Custer Scout*

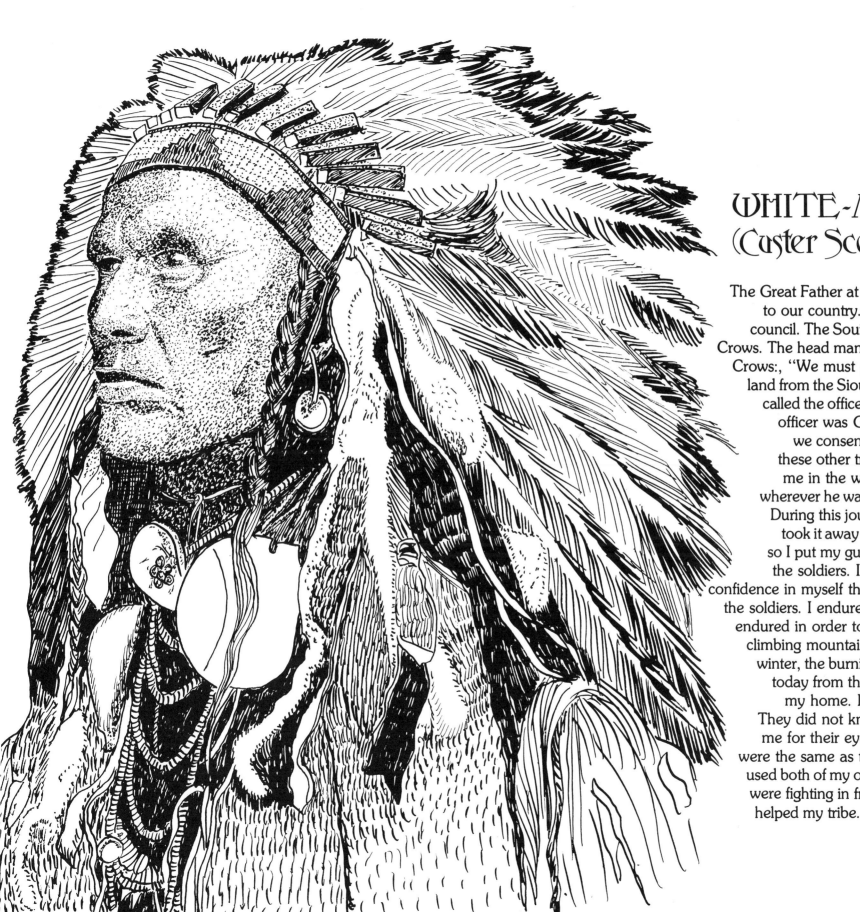

WHITE-MAN-RUNS-HIM
(Custer Scout): his account

The Great Father at Washington sent representatives out to our country. The Indians met them and held a council. The Souix were the hereditary enemies of the Crows. The head man sent by the Great Father said to the Crows:, "We must get together and fight, and get this land from the Sioux. We must win it by conquest." We called the officer, who was lame, No-Hip-Bone—the officer was General Terry. We loved our land so we consented to go in with the soldiers and put these other tribes off the land. No-Hip-Bone took me in the winter time, and I went with him wherever he wanted me to go until the next summer. During this journey I had a good horse. The Sioux took it away from me, and I was left to go on foot, so I put my gun on my shoulder and marched with the soldiers. I thought that I was a man, and had confidence in myself that I was right. And so I kept up with the soldiers. I endured all the hardships the soldiers endured in order to hold my land. We had hardships climbing mountains, fording rivers, frost and cold of winter, the burning heat of summer—my bones ache today from the exposure, but it was all for love of my home. I stood faithfully by the soldiers. They did not know the country. I did. They wanted me for their eye; they could not see. The soldiers were the same as though they were blind, and I used both of my own eyes for them. The soldiers and I were fighting in friendship, what they said, I did. So I helped my tribe.

123

Land is a very valuable thing, and especially our land. I knew the Cheyennes and Sioux wanted to take it by conquest, so I stayed with the soldiers to help hold it. No-Hip-Bone moved to Tongue River at the time the leaves were getting full. We heard that General Custer was coming and I and thirty soldiers went down the river in boats. Two scouts, Elk and Two-Whistles, were with me. At the junction of the Yellowstone with the Missouri River we met Custer. I was the first one of the Crows to shake hands with General Custer. He gripped me by the hand tight and said: "You are the One I want to see, and I am glad that you are first." We went into the steamboat with General Custer, and he pointed out different places to me as objects of interest. I directed Custer up to No-Hip-Bone, who had moved to the mouth of the Little Rosebud. They had a council; Bonnie Bravo was their interpreter. General Custer said to the interpreter, pointing to me: "This is the kind of man we want for this campaign, and I want some others also."

Goes-Ahead, Hairy Moccasin, White Swan, Paints-His-Face-Yellow, and Curly were chosen. There were six of us altogether. The others were sent back. We always moved ahead of Custer—we were his pilots. We always traveled at night, climbing the mountains and wading the rivers. During the day we made a concealed camp. We traveled in this way several days before we reached the Sioux camp. When we reached the top of the Wolf Mountains we saw the enemy's camp near where the Custer Field is at the present time. Hairy Moccasin, Goes-Ahead, Curly, and myself saw the camp. Custer had halted at the foot of a mountain, and we all went back and told Custer that we had seen a big camp, and it was close. Custer was rejoiced and anxious to go ahead and make the battle. The sun was just peeping when we saw

the camp. It was eight or nine o'clock when we scouts all went ahead again. We got close to the place of the enemy's camp, and Custer divided the scouts, sent some across the river, and the others remained on the hill.

In the meantime Custer had divided his command. Yellow Face and White Swan went with Reno across the river; Goes-Ahead, Hairy Moccasin, Curly, and myself remained with Custer. Custer sent me to a high knoll. He said, "Go and look for me and see where I can make a success." He left it to me. When I was up there I looked around and the troops were very close upon me, and I motioned to them to come on, and we passed up on to the ridge. The Indian scouts stood in front of Custer and led his men. We went down to the Little Horn until we came to a little coulee, and were moving towards the enemy's camp. We wanted to cross the river at that place. The Sioux fired at us. We then went up the hill to the ridge. I was all along the ridge where the fight was raging. We looked over the river, and saw Reno in his engagement with the Sioux. Finally they wiped out Reno, and he retreated to the hills.

Custer and all of us got off our horses here. At that time the enemy was surrounding us. They were banging away at us. We had a heavy skirmish. Custer then came up and said: "You have done your duty. You have led me to the enemy's camp. And now the thing for you to do is to obey my orders and get away." Farther up the river was a packtrain, escorted by three red soldiers, and I made my way to the packtrain, and I found the Indians there fighting. Custer when he told me to go said: "You go; I am now going with my boys." Had Custer not ordered me to go, the people who visit the Custer Field today would see my name on the monument. When I got back to the packtrain, I directed them back to where the old trenches are today, and where you may still see a pile of bones. The Indians had killed all the mules when I got there.

The fight lasted through the whole of a long, hot summer day. My friends, the soldiers who were with Custer, were all wiped out. When the sun went down I was about exhausted and I had no clothes on save a breechcloth. All the scouts were dressed like myself. When night came on, exhausted as we were, we scouts went down the river to meet No-Hip-Bone. We reached him early the next morning. There was a terrific rainstorm all night long. I had no clothes on and I stuck to my wet horse. My horse was so exhausted that he stumbled on through the night, and today I feel the effects of it. It was my nature to endure, but as strong as I was, it wounded me for life. We met No-Hip-Bone and told him that up the river yesterday, when the sun was midway between morning and noon, until the sun was midway between noon and night, the Indians had killed Custer and all of his command. And he was mad. We told him that our horses' hoofs were worn out and asked permission to go back home and get fresh horses. He said: "Yes, you can go, but come back. Meanwhile I will travel up the river and see the dead soldiers." I went to Pryor, our Crow camp.

Custer and the soldiers were my friends and companions, and I cried all night long as I rode through the rain to tell No-Hip-Bone the news.

When we were at the Rosebud, General Custer and his staff held a council as to what we should do when we found the enemy's camp, as to whether we should attack by day or night. I said we had better fight by night. Paints-His-Face-Yellow said: "Let us attack by day, so that we can see what we are doing." I thought I was laying a good plan for them but they listened to Yellow Face. General Custer was a brave and good man, a straightforward and honest man. When General Custer took me by the hand, patted me on the shoulder, and I looked him in the face, I said: "There is a good general." If General Custer was living today, I would get better treatment than I now receive. General Custer said: "Where does your tribe stay?" and I told him in the valley through which Pryor Creek runs, along the Big Horn River at Lodge Grass, and in the valley of the Little Horn—there is my home. Custer said: "If I die, you will get this land back and stay there, happy and contented, and if you die, you will be buried on your own land."

When I joined General Custer, I had full confidence in myself and my ability to help him, and for this reason I joined Custer so that I might help hold my land against our enemies, the Sioux and the Cheyennes. After the Custer battle, when we had obtained fresh horses, I took the other scouts with me, and we went over the field and looked at the remains of the dead soldiers who were my friends and companions. Knowing the country, I always directed General Custer to the best places to ford the river, and the easiest way to climb the hills, that he might reach the path of success. After the loss of my horse, I traveled on foot with the soldiers, and was willing even to go down to death with Custer in order that I might help him.

Taken down in Sept. 1909 by Dr. Joseph K. Dixon, and published in *The Vanishing Race.*

GOES-AHEAD (Custer Scout): his account

I was under General Terry at the Yellowstone at the mouth of the Big Horn. There was a boat at the mouth of the Big Horn. The steamboat had a pontoon bridge reaching to the shore. The soldiers came off the boat and joined General Terry's command. Then General Terry gave the command for us all to mount and go ahead of the line. Then he selected men from this line of scouts to send to General Custer as scouts. He mentioned my name and also called Yellow Shield, White-Man-Runs-Him, White Swan, Hairy Moccasin, and Curly out of this line. There were six of us. Then they gave us orders to go on the steamboat. We sailed down to the mouth of the Little Rosebud, where we got off the boat. Then we went into General Custer's tent; we sat on one side of the tent, and that was the day of great pleasure to me. I saw that General Custer was a man of about six feet two inches, slim and well-built, and kind-hearted. He wore long hair. General Custer told us that he had heard that the Crow Indians were the bravest scouts and the best horsemen among all the Indians, and that was the reason he had asked General Terry to send us to him. He said he had some Mandan scouts but they were not going to do any Indian scouting for him, but would remain in the line and do the cooking for the scouts. Then General Custer told us he wanted us to find the Sioux trail and follow it until we reached the Sioux camp and to report to him where they were. He did not want us to enter into battle with the Sioux, but to come back and tell him the location of their camp. Then after he had won the battle he would give us all the Sioux horses we could drive home.

Then we scouted in search of the Sioux. We followed the trail of the Sioux where they had been moving, and we got to where they had camped on the Little Rosebud. I got to the place where they had been camping just after their fight with General Crook at the battle of Little

Rosebud, and they had moved to the Little Big Horn. General Custer gave us strict orders when we were scouting not to mistake the scouts of General Terry and General Crook for the other Indians, because we might run across them and to be sure we had seen the Sioux. We were two nights on our way before we came upon the village. It was located on the plain above where the Custer fight took place, on the banks of the Little Big Horn. I was by myself and after I saw the village I went back and reported to General Custer and he was greatly pleased. I always tried to obey and follow closely my instructions. I reported to General Custer that it was a pretty big village. Custer said, "That is just what I am looking for; we might just as well enter the battle." General Custer told me to go ahead of his column, and keep ahead, but not to go too far for fear the enemy would capture me, and I did what he ordered me to do.

General Custer marched his troops all night up to a point about five miles from where I reported to him, and then he divided his command. Reno followed down the Reno Creek, Custer crossed the ridge, going over to the Medicine Tail Creek which runs into the Little Big Horn. There on the creek General Custer dismounted, and said prayers to the Heavenly Father. Then he rose and shook hands with me, and said: "My scout, if we win the battle, you will be one of the noted men of the Crow Nation." In a moment or two he turned around again and said to me: "I have forgotten to tell you, you are not to fight in this battle, but to go back and save your life." White-Man-Runs-Him and Hairy Moccasin and Curly heard what Custer said. The other two were with Reno. We were in the sight of the camp when Custer told us this. Reno had then crossed the Little Big Horn with his two Crow scouts and the rest of the Mandans. If we had been smart enough we would have asked General Custer to give us a paper as a recommendation, but we did not know anything much in those days.

As we stood looking, we saw Reno take his battle position between eight and nine o'clock. Custer stood there a little for we expected all the Crow, Creeks, and Terry's command, to meet us there that day, and make a battle that day. After he said this Custer started into the battle and opened fire on the camp. We scouts were up on top of the bluff, and we fired at the camp. Hairy Moccasin and White-Man-Runs-Him were with him. Curly I did not see because he carried the last dispatch to Reno. Although Custer had given us command to do no fighting, it was impossible for us to stand there on the bluff and see the soldiers fighting and not do something, so we had to fire. I do not want to make any mistake in this story, and I have told the truth. Reno took the battle. There was so much smoke and dust that I could hardly tell, but Reno was driven back by the Indians toward the bluff. In all the valley and woods there was nothing but Indians. Then I did not know which way he went, for I was fighting my own way. Custer also opened fire just beyond Medicine Creek where he had crossed. Soon after Reno opened fire Custer began his fire. From there I cannot tell you. About four or five o'clock the packtrain came up and the hard fighting was down there. I went back to the packtrain and helped fight a while and then I took to the pine hills away over to the east. When I heard that Custer had been killed I said: "He is a man to fight the enemy. He loved to fight, but if he fights and is killed, he will have to be killed."

Taken down in Sept. 1909 by Dr. Joseph K. Dixon, and published in *The Vanishing Race.*

"... up there, where the fight took place, where the last stand was made, the Long Hair stood like a sheaf of wheat with all the ears fallen around him .... He killed a man when he fell. He laughed .... He had fired his last shot."

—*Sitting Bull*

The question of who killed Custer was never answered. A symbolic encounter between Custer and Crazy Horse painted by Kills Two is reproduced on the facing page. The Indians at the Battle at the Little Big Horn River generally thought they were being attacked by Crook or by a unit of his regiment because they had been attacked by him only three months previously. They could not have recognized Custer by his long hair (Hi-es-tzie), as he had cut it off before the battle. They probably were able to identify him after the battle because, as a great enemy chief, he had not been scalped or mutilated.

128

General Custer.

Crazy Horse

"The next morning I was at General Terry's camp and reported. . . . I could not speak English and there were no interpreters there, so I took the grass and piled it all up in a heap, then I took my fingers and scattered it wide apart, and attempted in this way to show General Terry that the soldiers were all killed."

—*Curly, Custer Scout*

CURLY (Custer Scout): his account

We had been brought to the Little Rosebud down the Yellowstone by steamer. After we had landed we were told to get dinner, dress ourselves, paint up, and get ready to scout. Then we heard that General Custer wanted to use us. We mounted and rode over to General Custer's camp. He had a big tent. We got off at the door. I was the first to shake his hand. I had a dollar in my hand, and I pressed that into his hand. Each scout shook hands with him. When I saw Custer sitting there, tall and slim, with broad shoulders and kind eyes, I said to myself: "There is a kind, brave, and thinking man." The first words that Custer uttered were: "I have seen all the tribes but the Crows, and now I see them for the first time, and I think they are good and brave scouts. I have some scouts here, but they are worthless. I have heard that the Crows are good scouts, and I have sent for you to come to my command, I have given General Terry six hundred dollars for the use of you Crow Indians as scouts. I have called you Indians here not to fight but to trace the enemy and tell me where they are; I do not want you to fight. You find the Indians and I will do the fighting. With all these dollars I have given you I want you to go into the steamboat and buy some shirts and paint. We will leave here in two days. We will follow the Little Rosebud up." That evening the Mandans danced with us, and they gave us some money. Then Custer said: "I think you are good Indians. I will have the cook prepare our dinner, and you can eat alongside of me. I will have a a tent put up here and you can camp near me."

Within two days we started on our journey. We got on our horses and started with Custer up the

Little Rosebud. The whole command were with us. He asked us where was the last Sioux camp while we were scouting for Terry. We told him we would not be near there until tomorrow. The next morning we were at the place where we saw the last camp of the Sioux. Then we followed the Sioux trail. We found the trail, and saw that it forked on the Little Rosebud River. Custer gave orders for Goes-Ahead to follow one trail, and for me to follow the other to see which was the largest camp. We found that the trails came together after a while and that the Sioux were all in one camp. When we got to the camp, we saw that a battle had been fought, for we found the scalps and beards of white men.

We went back that night and reported to Custer. It was pretty late, but Custer's cook was up and had a light in his tent. Then Custer told the cook to give the boys their meal. After we got through our supper we went to his tent as Custer wanted to see us. We took with us some of the scalps and white men's beards, and showed them to Custer. Then Custer asked us if the camp separated or came together, and we told him it came together. Then Custer said: "This is the main point—these Sioux have been killing white people, and I have been sent here by the Great Father to conquer them and bring them back to their reservation. I am a great chief, but I do not know whether I will get through this summer alive or dead. There will be nothing more good for the Sioux—if they massacre me, they will still suffer, and if they do not kill me, they will still suffer for they have disobeyed orders. I do not know whether I will pass through this battle or not, but if I live, I will recommend you boys and you will be leaders of the Crows. Tomorrow I want five of my Crow boys to go on the trail.''

We started just before daybreak. When we started we saw some of the Mandans running round on the top of the hill, and Goes-Ahead told me to go back and tell the command that they must not have these Mandans running round over the hills, but to keep them down in the valley, as we might be near the Sioux camp and would be discovered before we knew it. Then they ordered these Mandans to come down from the hills and stay down. When I started back I heard a howl like a coyote. White Swan, Hairy Moccasin, Goes-Ahead, and White-Man-Runs-Him were coming to report. The Sioux had broken camp the day before and had camped above where their old camp was on the Little Rosebud. Custer told us to go on ahead and see which way they went, and we came to where they had broken camp. We followed the trail until we saw that they had camped on the Little Horn, and then we noticed that the Sioux had gone toward the Little Horn and we waited at the head of Tallec Creek for the command to come up. The command did not come up, for they had camped on the Little Rosebud; and we went back to the camp. Then the scouts had an argument, and I went by myself and asked Custer what we should do. Custer asked me what I came back for. I told him that the trail of the Sioux had gone to the west, toward the Little Horn, and that I had come back for further orders. Then Custer told me to get my supper, and take a lunch for the other scouts, and take with me two soldiers and go on and camp where the Sioux were located.

I got up and saw them through the smoke. The command came halfway toward us and then stopped and this officer who was with us wrote a message for General Custer, and sent a Mandan scout back with it. Custer did not wait. As soon as he got the message his men moved on rapidly toward the Custer Field. Then Custer said: "We will charge upon them now—that settles their journey." Custer then gave the order to inspect their guns. Soon they started on down the ridge. Custer told us to go on ahead. We followed the creek all the way down. There was half a battalion behind us. We found a tepee like the one in which we are now sitting, as we went along, and found two dead Sioux inside. Then the main command came up to us. We all stopped at the fork of the Little Reno Creek. Custer split up his command at this point, and told Reno to follow the creek down, which is now called Reno Creek. Then we crossed over the ridge. I came down with Custer as far as the creek; then he gave me a message to take to Reno. I did not know the import of the message. I brought the answer back from Reno to Custer.

While I was delivering the last message, Reno was fighting his battle, but it was not very fierce, and when I got to Custer with the message he was fighting at the mouth of the creek. Then Custer told me to go and save my life. I made a circle around, and I found that my ammunition was getting low. I found a dead Sioux. I took his ammunition and gun and horse, and got out. I stayed near where the dead Sioux was until the fight was pretty fierce. I went up on a high butte to the east of the battlefield where I could see the fight. When I got on the high hill I looked back, and saw that Custer was the last man to stand. After that I rushed over the hill and hid in the brush. The next morning about five or six o'clock I was in General Terry's camp and reported. General Terry called his officers about him. I could not speak English and there were no intrepreters there, so I took the grass and piled it all up in a heap, then I took my fingers and scattered it wide apart, and attempted in this way to show General Terry that the soldiers were all killed. Then General Terry gave me a dispatch. I was very tired and did not want to go, but I had to take this dispatch from General Terry to Reno at the packtrain. Reno gave me a dispatch to take back to Terry, while they were burying the dead soldiers. Then another dispatch was given me to take to the head command at the steamboat. I felt sorry and depressed that I should never again see Custer.

Taken down in Sept. 1909 by Dr. Joseph K. Dixon, and published in *The Vanishing Race.*

Custer is the largest figure in the central group, holding a pistol.

CUSTER'S LAST FIGHT by White Bird
—Courtesy West Point Museum

These drawings by Amos Bad Heart Buffalo show the end of Custer's command, with Crazy Horse killing the General in the first (center left) with a battle axe. The inscription (top left): "Last of General Custer, June 26, 1876." The last trooper alive is shown escaping at bottom right. On the following page is shown the same trooper hotly pursued, while at lower right, captured horses are being held. The trooper shoots himself to escape torture, but would probably have been spared as it is a tradition among the Sioux that the last warrior shall not be killed.

In the last drawing, the pursuers have caught up with the body. One warrior has captured his horse, and leads it by the reins while the Indian on the far right shoots arrows into the body. No scalp has been taken because the Indians considered a suicide untouchable. The inscription in Lakota (on top) means that this was the end of Custer's command. It also says that "the long guns taken away from them were counted, and it is said they numbered more than seven hundred." (This would mean from both Custer's and Reno's command.)

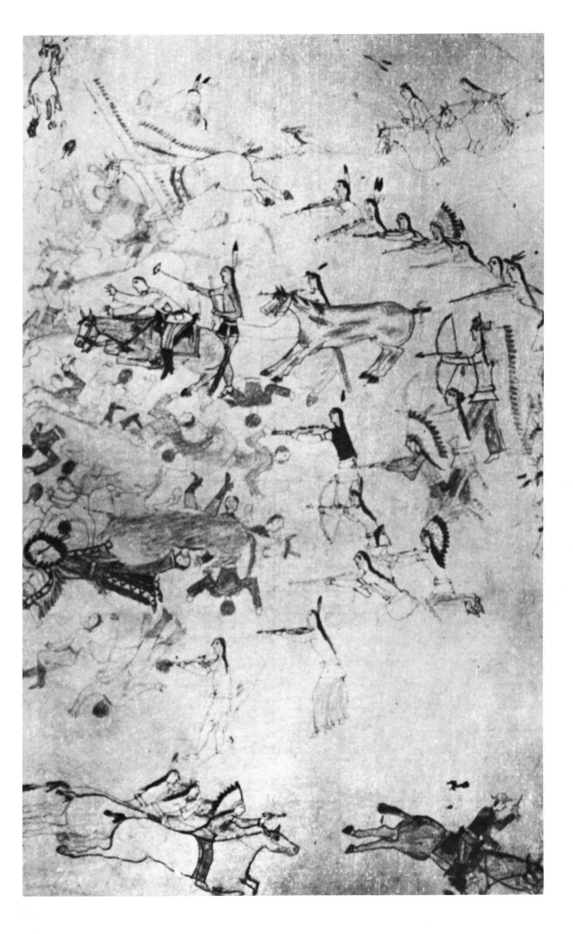

Indians leaving the battleground, leading their captive horses, as painted by Amos Bad Heart Buffalo (*above*) and Red Horse (*facing page*). Red Horse had a very different style from all the other painters.

"Enough! Henala! Enough!" my uncle (Sitting Bull) shouted. "Those soldiers are trying to live, let them live. Let them go. If we kill all of them, a bigger army will march against us."
—*Henry Oscar One Bull*

INDIANS LEAVING BATTLEGROUND by Red Horse—
Courtesy of Custer Battlefield Nat. Monument Museum

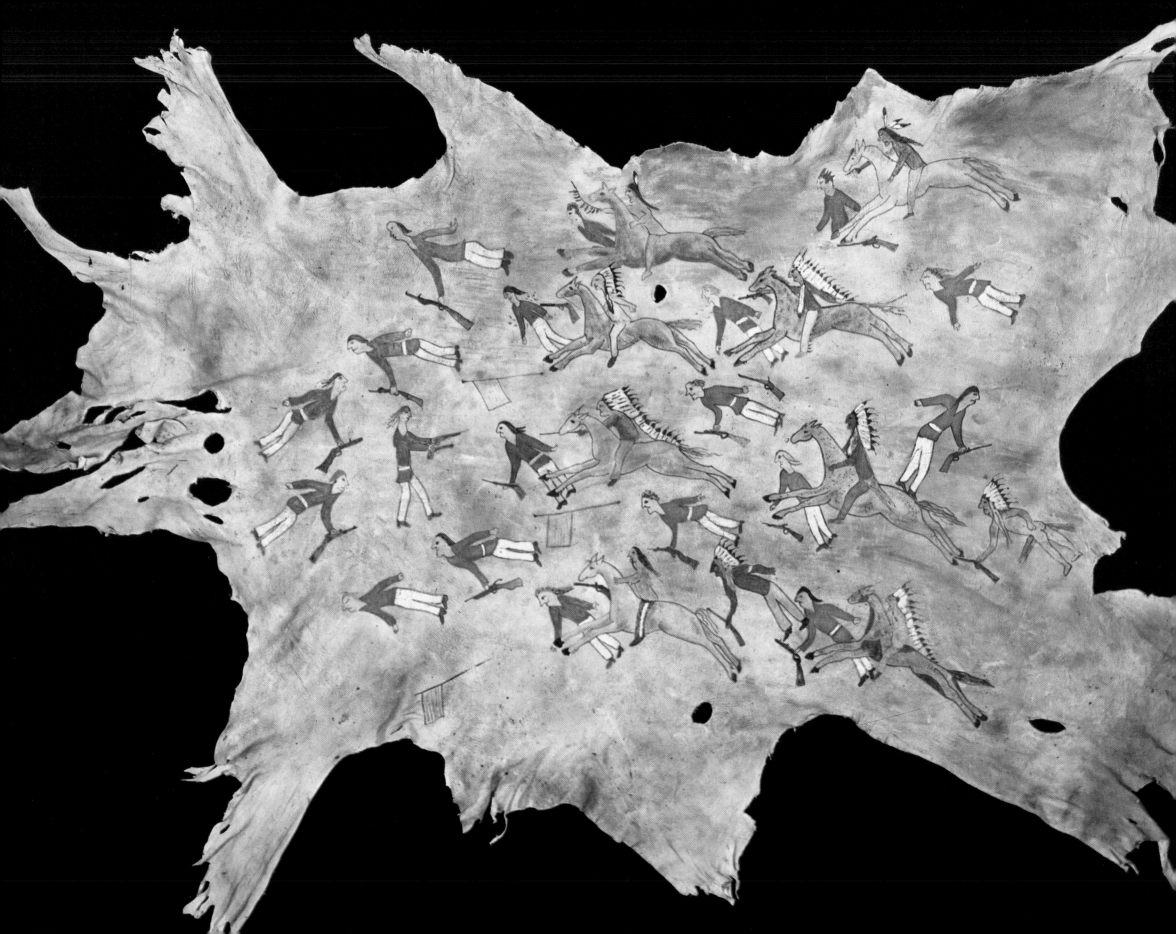

THE AFTERMATH OF THE BATTLE

Author's copy of deerskin painted by Lame Deer, Northern Cheyenne, with record of Custer's Battle at the Little Big Horn. It depicts the battle's aftermath, showing the soldiers' bodies in the floating position that was used to denote their spirits descending.

Courtesy of Museum of the American Indian, Heye Foundation

Picture from the Southwest Museum

Sometime in 1898, the artist Frederick Remington asked Kicking Bear, a veteran of the Battle at the Little Big Horn River, to paint his version of the event. When completed, it was very much in the style of the old pictographs, and clearly, Kicking Bear's personal version. Custer can be seen in his very yellow buckskins at left center. He had cut his hair short before the battle, but Kicking Bear pictures him as his Indian name—Long Hair (Hi-es-tzie).

The soldiers in outline, rising at the left top, are the departing spirits of the dead soldiers.

The four figures standing in the center are from left to right: Sitting Bull, Rain-in-the-Face, Crazy Horse, and the artist, Kicking Bear, whose footsteps are seen tracking around the Indian army scout he had killed in the battle. The wigwams of the Indian encampment are at the bottom left, with the squaws preparing the victory dance for their warrior husbands' return. Note the U.S. flag in the hands of one of them.

143

The Shoshone War Dance, painted by Charles Washakie on muslin (*right*). This kind of dance was performed by the victors of the Battle at the Little Big Horn. The figure at the top right holds the wolfskin symbol of war. This was a dance for men only.

Custer's dead cavalry as drawn by Red Horse appears on the facing page. Custer is probably the unstripped and unmutilated figure without a beard in the middle left of the picture, lying diagonally across the other soldiers. All the Indians seem to agree that Custer was not touched in death.

"The wise men and chiefs of our nation gave out to our people not to mutilate the dead white chief, for he was a brave warrior and died a brave man, and his remains should be respected."
—*Low Dog*

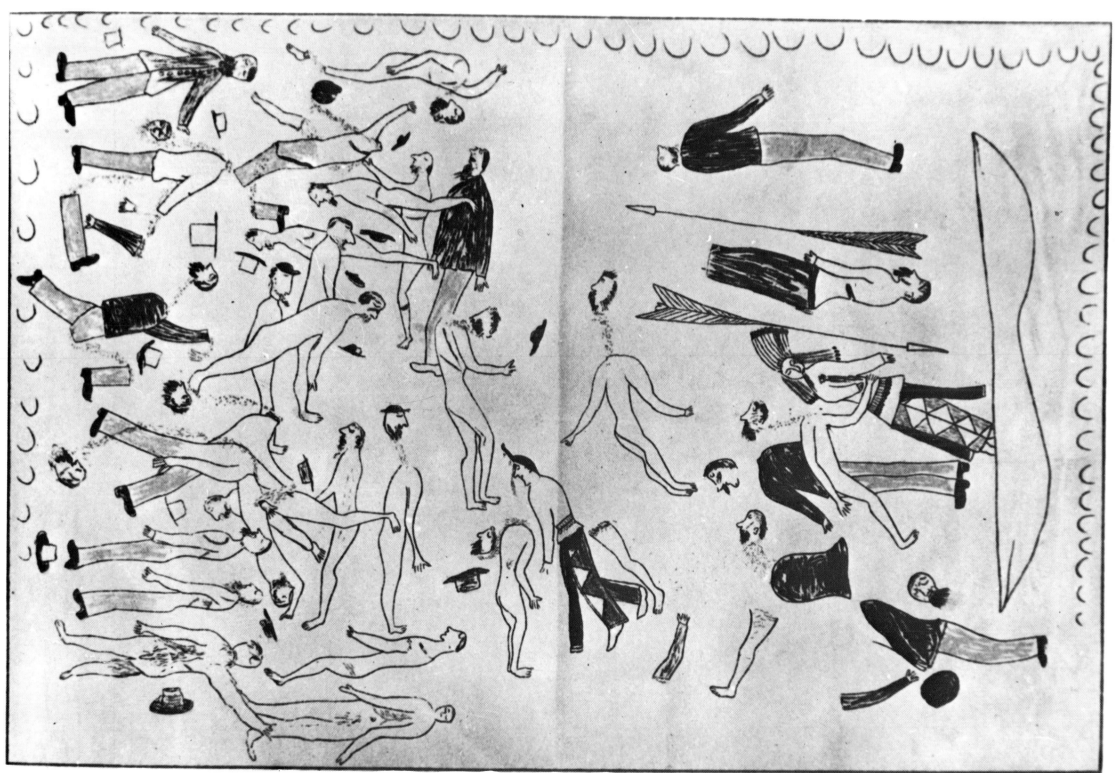

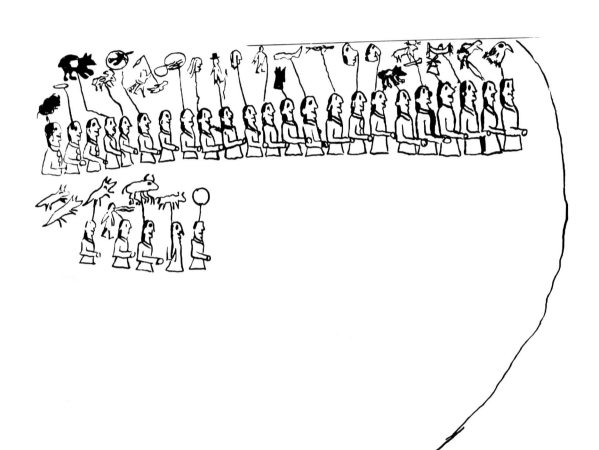

PAPER № 1.

Boston.

PAPER № 2.

After the Battle at the Little Big Horn River, Sitting Bull and some of his band sought to escape the army by hiding out in Canada. The U.S. Government sent their representatives to lure him back within their jurisdiction by inviting him to a peace meeting in Boston.

Sitting Bull avoided the obvious trap by refusing to attend. One of his band (unknown) drew these satirical sketches in 1877 to show his idea of what might have taken place had the great medicine man been foolish enough to go to Boston.

Paper #1 shows Sitting Bull (in the top row, farthest left) sitting in Canada with his band while the liason man Howling Wolf talks with the commissioners in Boston.

Paper #2 shows General A. Terry (marked with a star), the enemy of Sitting Bull, wracked by anguish and chagrin after the imagined conference. He goes crazy and rushes into an open grave prepared for him.

drawing by an anonymous companion of Sitting Bull; from the National Archives

147

Wanaji Wacipi Oskayate.

Three Ghost Dancers wearing the typical costumes of the dance are drawn in the picture on the facing page. The religious symbols of the moon, the four-pointed star, and the dragonfly can be seen in the shawl worn by the left figure. The translation of the Lakota inscription on the right is by Helen Blish, and reads:

Our Father saw the common people mourning the world over. For this reason he took pity on them. He was among the people long ago and said that the people should gather together. He presented himself in person and taught them a dance, and told them what costume to wear. And he told them to live peaceably. But then the Indians went too far, and a great many died, so he did not wait for them. They have now forgotten it.

The revival of the Ghost Dance ritual was the last hope of the Plains Indians, virtually imprisoned, and starving because all the buffalo had been killed off. A Paiute named Wovoka, a messiah, preached the ritual which asked the spirits of all dead Indians to bring the buffalo back and to cause the disappearance of the white men. James Mooney described the Dance in a report published in 1896:

"All the songs are adapted to the simple measure of the dance step . . . the dancers moving from right to left, following the course of the sun . . . hardly lifting the feet from the ground . . . Each song is started in the same manner, first in an undertone while singers stand still in their places, and then with full voice as they begin to circle around. At intervals between the songs . . . the dancers unclasp hands and sit down to smoke or talk for a few minutes . . . There is no limit to the number of these songs, as every trance at every dance produces a new one. . . . Thus a single dance may easily result in twenty or thirty songs."

pp. 133–134, James Mooney, *The Ghost Dance Religion and the Sioux Outbreak of 1890* (Bureau of American Ethnology, Fourteenth Annual Report, 1896)

Wovoka's own dance was described by a Northern Cheyenne follower named Porcupine:

"They cleared off a space in the form of a circus ring and we all gathered there . . . . The Christ (i.e. Wovoka) was with them . . . . I looked around to find him, and finally saw him sitting on one side of the ring . . . . They made a big fire to throw light on him . . . He sat with his head bowed all the time. After a while he rose and said he was very glad to see his children . . . "My children, I want you to listen to all I have to say to you. I will teach you, too, how to dance a dance, and I want you to dance it. Get ready for your dance and then, when the dance is over, I will talk to you." He was dressed in a white coat with stripes. The rest of his dress was a white man's except that he had on a pair of moccasins. Then he commenced the dance, everybody joining in, the Christ singing while we danced . . . (Later) he commenced to tremble all over, violently for a while, and then sat down. We danced all that night, the Christ lying down beside us apparently dead."

Porcupine's description from *The Winged Serpent: An Anthology of American Indian Prose and Poetry* (The John Day Co., N.Y., 1946)

The Ghost Dance, as drawn by Amos Bad Heart Buffalo. In the center right, the English inscription reads, "Ghost Dance Sept. 1890." The men and women dancers border the drawing. The upper center shows the sacred tree with sacrifice banners attached. Sacred pipes are crossed at its base. Below the tree is a man in a trance. The two figures right of center, one standing with arms outstretched, are both apparently in a trance.

The words of the Ghost Dance song in both Lakota and English are in the left half of the drawing:

ATE HEYELO	THIS THE FATHER SAY
CAN NUPA WAN CICICA UPI CA	HE BRING THE PIPE FOR YOU
YANI PI KTE WA	AND YOU WILL LIVE
ATE HEYELO ATE HEYELO	THIS THE FATHER SAY
	THIS THE FATHER SAY

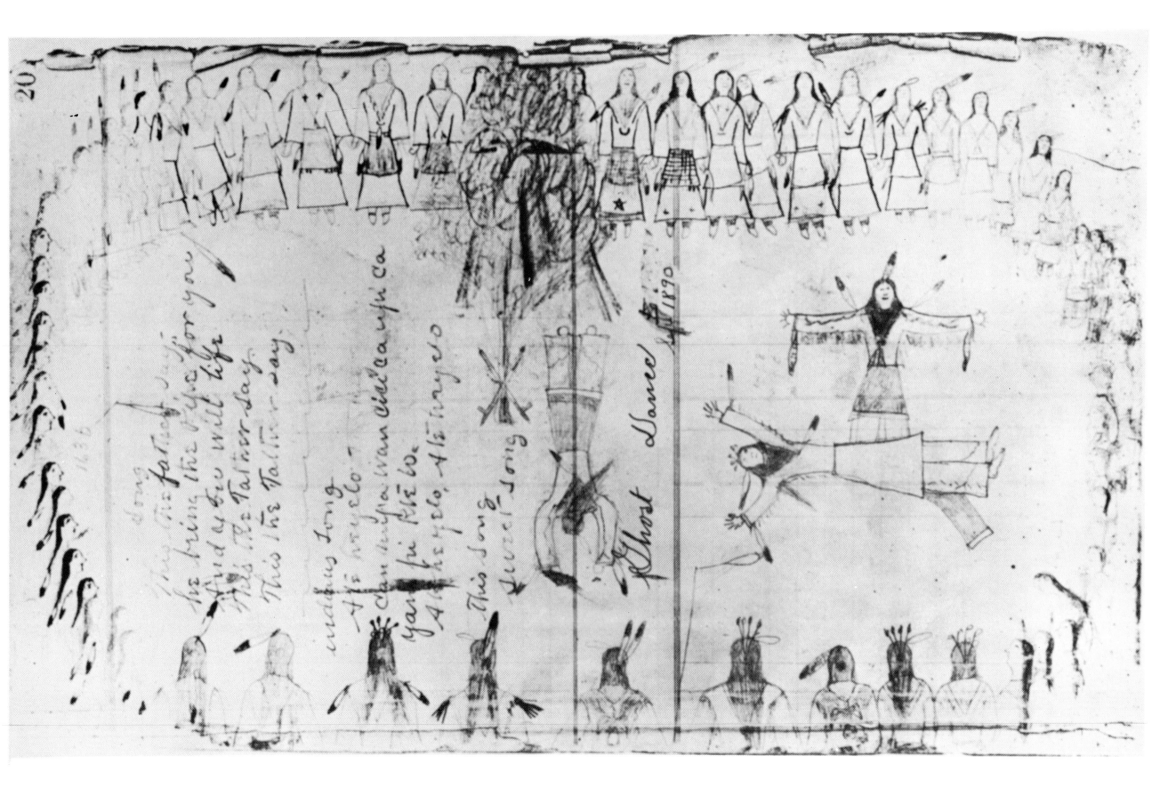

Amos Bad Heart Buffalo's drawing of the death of his cousin Crazy Horse. The Lakota, translated by Helen Blish reads:

In the season of 1887 Crazy Horse was killed. A Lakota seized him. His name was Little Big Man. The soldiers and scouts used guns on him. They asked him to go to Washington, but he refused. For this he was killed. Notes in English: Indian Chief Crazy Horse at Fort Robinson, Nebr. White River.

The minute figures stretching in rows across the bottom of the drawing are crowds of Indians and their horses waiting outside the fort. Amos's version of deliberate slaughter is the general one held by most Indians. However, Helen Blish, in her manuscript, gives another account as follows:

"The story of two Indians of good repute who were on duty at the time do not confirm the implications of this drawing, however. I give here the story of the Oglala scout Plenty Wolves, familiarly known and referred to in reports as Yankton Charley. His story is corroborated in every detail by that of Yellow Horse (Tasunke Hinzi), an Eastern Dakota son-in-law of Red Cloud. The two reports were secured independently (by John Corloff).

"Crazy Horse had been arrested and was brought in to the fort. There he was asked to go to Washington to talk over the situation of his people and himself with a view to settlement of difficulties. He refused and reached for the revolver in his holster. Fortunately, Plenty Wolves had just removed the weapon. Crazy Horse did manage, however, to get his knife before the guards could seize his arms. Little Big Man (Wicasa Tankala), the Indian scout on his right, realized the futility of the chief's opposition and appealed to him, calling him 'nephew' (a truly appealing manner of speech of the Dakotas), to take the whole matter calmly. But the captive would not listen.

"Knife drawn, Crazy Horse struggled with the two guards. The soldier placed on guard behind him, with drawn bayonet, backed away to avoid touching the Indian with his bayonet. He moved back so far that, without his realizing it, the butt of his rifle almost touched the wall. A sudden, violent struggle on the part of the captive threw him heavily against the bayonet. Of course, the result was fatal; the blade was run through his body."

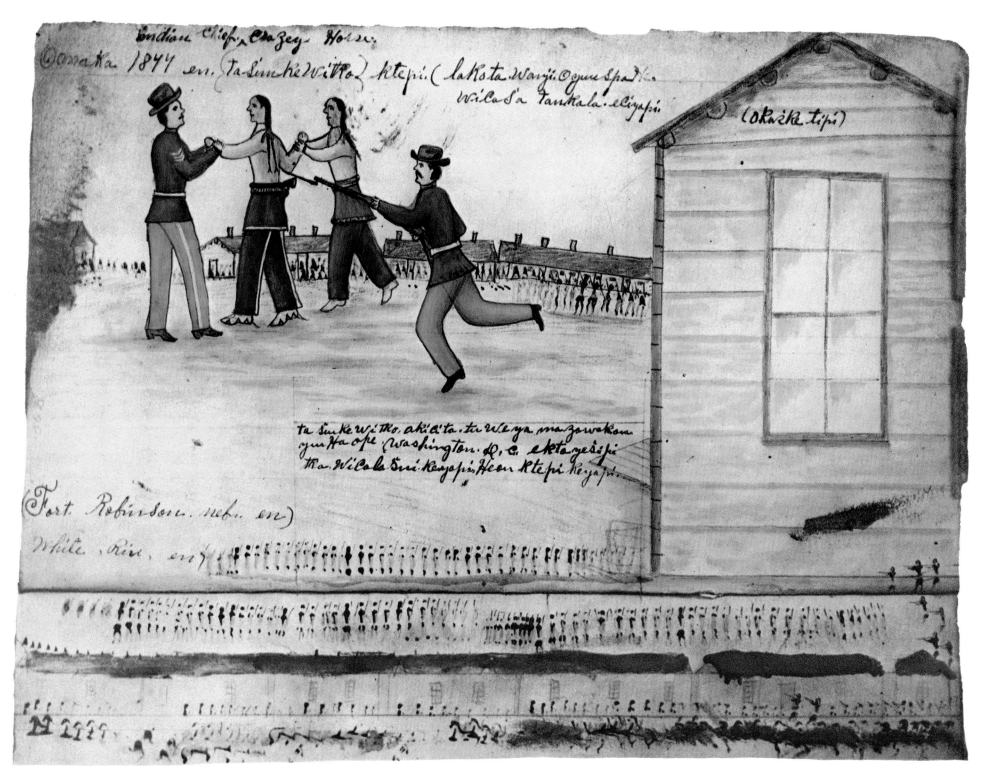

Indian Chief, Crazy Horse;

Omaha 1877 en (Ta Sun ke Witko) ktepi (lakota wanji Ogue Spa) ka
Wicasa Tankala eliyapi

(okicize tipi)

ta Sun ke Witko, aki'ci'ta tu wie ya mazowakon
yu Ha ope (washington. D.C. ektagesipi
ka Wicala Sui keyapi Heon ktepi keyapi.

(Fort Robinson, nebr. en)

White River, en

The death of Sitting Bull and his son (1890) can only be viewed as part of the Wounded Knee episode. The Ghost Dance ritual swept the Plains Indians with a frenzied hope. The army feared it would lead to war again and as Sitting Bull was still the titular head of the Plains Indians, they saw to it that the Indian police killed him and his son, Crow Foot. This scene shows Sitting Bull in his home at Standing Rock, and the son being shot in his bed. The top inscription in English reads, "Sitting Bull"; at bottom, "Standing Rock, North Dakota," followed by the Lakota "EN" for "at" or "in." The Lakota translated says, "Crow Foot was killed in his sleep" and "In the season of 1890, Sitting Bull was killed at his home."

154

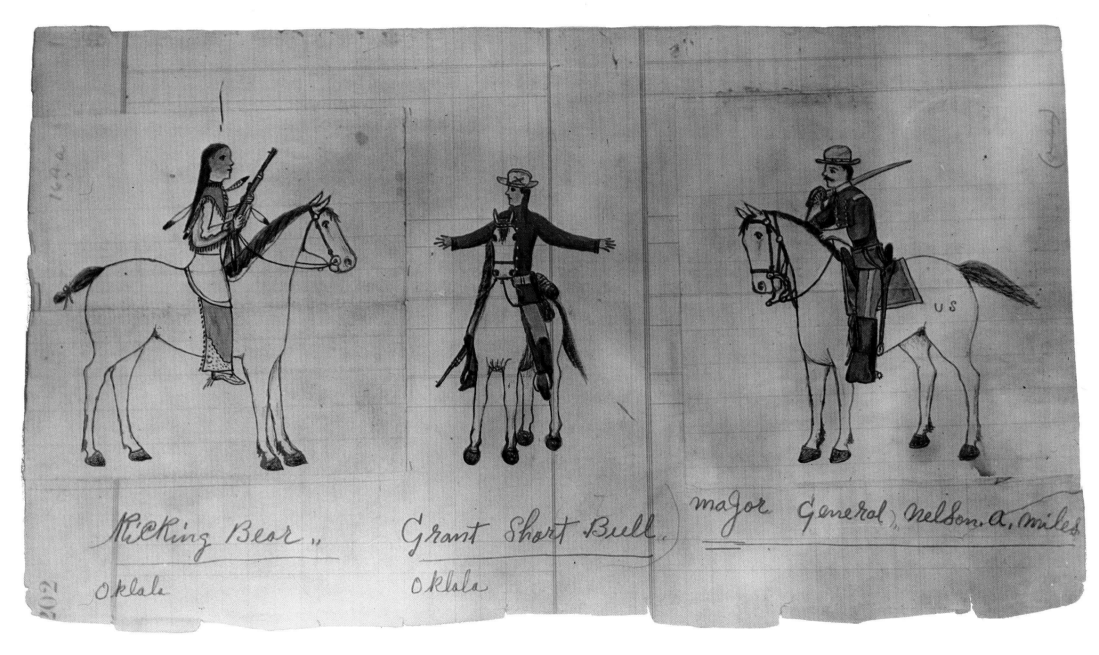

A symbolic meeting depicting Grant Short Buffalo (Grant Short Bull), the Oglala Sioux Scout (center), as mediator. Kicking Bear (Mato Wamatka), representing the Oglala Sioux, wears a Ghost Dance costume (left). At right is General Nelson A. Miles.

155

Amos Bad Heart Buffalo shows the moment just before the attempted disarming of the men at Wounded Knee Creek, some of whom are squatting in the center smoking pipes, and some standing amidst the women and children. The Indians are shown surrounded by a circle of infantrymen with raised rifles, who are backed up by an outer ring of cavalry. The four Hotchkiss machine guns that were trained and used on the Indians are not shown. The translation by Helen Blish of the Lakota inscription at the right is, "This refers to the killing of Big Foot. This was worse than the Custer battle. They even killed a great many children." The scene on the facing page shows the actual massacre a few moments later.

156

157

By 1890, Washington policy was divided between advocates of outright genocide and those who, more moderately, were for driving the remaining Plains Indians onto reservations. This latter course of action was to be facilitated by a policy of deliberate starvation. The policy to be followed depended largely upon local circumstances.

Big Foot and his followers escaped from their reservation to join in a large meeting of Ghost Dance ritualists. They were caught and driven to Wounded Knee Creek, where local circumstances could not have been worse. They were surrounded by the reformed Seventh Cavalry (Custer's) who sought any pretext for revenge and slaughter.

General Miles himself tried to have the cavalrymen responsible brought to trial, but his move was quashed. Instead, twenty-three Medals of Honor were given out to the heroes of the massacre.

Dewey Beard graphically describes the horror of the massacre as he remembers it:

"That is another time I will never forget. It was the last night on earth for my first wife and family. Next morning the soldiers surrounded us and ordered us to give up our weapons. They even took away our skinning knives. But we were not looking for war and wanted to do as the soldiers ordered.

"One Indian's gun was fired by accident. I heard later it belonged to Sitting Bull's deaf-mute son, who couldn't hear the order to disarm. After that shot, the soldiers let loose with everything they had. Unarmed, we didn't have a chance. Men, women, even babies were shot down. Soldiers galloped after those who ran and cut them down with sabers. Then they opened up on us with cannons (Hotchkiss guns) and pounded everything flat—tepees, people, even horses and dogs. I was struck by bullets in my arm, chest, and leg, but I ran limping down a gulley and got away.

"Hiding in a cutbank, I looked back at the camp. My wife and child were lying there motionless. A few paces away were my old mother and father, my sister, and, beyond them, my two younger brothers. All of them were dead. I waited there in the snow beside the cutbank and prayed for death."

INDEX